THE
BRITISH
LITERARY
BALLAD

A Study in
Poetic Imitation

G. Malcolm Laws, Jr.

SOUTHERN ILLINOIS UNIVERSITY PRESS
Carbondale and Edwardsville

Feffer & Simons, Inc.
London and Amsterdam

Dedicated
to the memory of
William Harvey Marshall
Colleague and Friend

ACKNOWLEDGMENTS

*E*XCERPTS from "Miss Gee" and "Victor" reprinted with permission of Faber and Faber Ltd. and Random House, Inc. from *Collected Shorter Poems 1927–1957* by W. H. Auden © Copyright 1966, 1965, 1960, 1959, 1958, 1957, 1955, 1954, 1953, 1952, 1951, 1950, 1949, 1947, 1946, 1945, 1941, 1940, 1938, 1937, 1934 by W. H. Auden. Copyright, 1937, by Random House, Inc. Copyright, 1934, by The Modern Library, Inc. Copyright renewed, 1961, 1964, by W. H. Auden.

Excerpts from John Betjeman's "A Subaltern's Love-Song" reprinted with permission of John Murray Ltd. and Houghton Mifflin Co. from *John Betjeman's Collected Poems.*

Excerpts from "The Water-Witch" reprinted with the permission of Burns & Oates Ltd. from *Complete Collected Ballads of Padraic Gregory (1912–1932).*

Excerpts from "Her Immortality," "The Dark-Eyed Gentleman," "Ah, Are You Digging on My Grave?" and "The Second Night" reprinted with permission of The Macmillan Company from *Collected Poems* by Thomas Hardy. Copyright 1925 by The Macmillan Company.

Excerpts from "The Mock Wife" and "The Forbidden Banns" reprinted with permission of The Macmillan Company from *Collected Poems* by Thomas Hardy. Copyright 1925 by The Macmillan Company, renewed 1953 by Lloyds Bank, Ltd.

Excerpts from "The Brother" and "The Catching Ballet of the Wedding Clothes" reprinted with permission of The Macmillan Company from *Winter Words* by Thomas Hardy. Copyright 1928 by Florence E. Hardy and Sydney E. Cockerell, renewed 1956 by Lloyds Bank, Ltd.

Excerpts from "Her Immortality," "The Dark-Eyed Gentleman," "Ah, Are You Digging on My Grave?" "The Second Night," "The Mock Wife," "The Forbidden Banns," "The Brother," and "The Catching Ballet of the Wedding Clothes" reprinted from *Collected Poems* by Thomas Hardy, by permission of the Hardy Estate; Macmillan London & Basingstoke; and The Macmillan Company of Canada Limited.

"Farewell to barn and stack and tree" and excerpts from "Bredon Hill," "The Carpenter's Son," and "The True Lover" from "A Shropshire Lad"—Authorised Edition—from *The Collected Poems of A. E. Housman.* Copyright 1938, 1940, © 1959 by Holt, Rinehart and Winston, Inc. Copyright © 1967, 1968 by Robert E. Symons. Reprinted by permission of Holt, Rinehart and Winston, Inc.; and also by permission of the Society of Authors as the literary representative of the Estate of A. E. Housman, and Jonathan Cape, Ltd., publishers of A. E. Housman's *Collected Poems.*

"Our Lady of the Sackcloth," copyright 1935 by Rudyard Kipling, "The Grave of the Hundred Head," "The Fall of Jock Gillespie," "The Sea-Wife," "The Ballad of the Bolivar," "The Gift of the Sea," "The Last Rhyme of True Thomas," "The Ballad of East and West," all from the book *Rudyard Kipling's Verse: Definitive Edition.* Reprinted by permission of Mrs. George Bambridge and Doubleday & Company, Inc.; and also by permission of Macmillan & Co., Ltd.

Excerpts from "The Streets of Laredo" reprinted with permission of Faber and Faber Ltd. and the Oxford University Press from *The Collected Poems of Louis MacNeice*, by Louis MacNeice.

Excerpts from "The Ballad of the Flood" reprinted with permission of Faber and Faber Ltd. and the Oxford University Press from *Collected Poems 1921–1958* by Edwin Muir.

Excerpts from John Crowe Ransom's introduction reprinted with permission of The Macmillan Company from *Selected Poems of Thomas Hardy* by John Crowe Ransom. © by The Macmillan Company, 1960, 1961.

Excerpts from "The Tower of St. Maur," reprinted from *The Collected Poems, Lyrical and Narrative* of A. Mary F. Robinson

(Madame Duclaux), London, 1902 by permission of Ernest Benn, Ltd., successors to T. Fisher Unwin.

I wish to thank Vernon Sternberg, the director, and his staff at the Southern Illinois University Press and especially Miss Elizabeth Wenning, my editor, for their gracious and efficient handling of this volume. And I am particularly grateful to Professor Tristram P. Coffin for a perceptive reading of the manuscript and always helpful comments and suggestions.

G. M. L., Jr.

Contents

———•—•———

Foreword

THE word *ballad* is used in so many different senses and contexts that any title which includes it is likely to be somewhat ambiguous. I am restricting the term to verse narratives that tell dramatic stories in conventionalized ways. Three classes of ballads must be broadly distinguished. Of these, the first two may be called the subliterary categories. The most familiar is that of the folk ballads or popular ballads, traditional narrative songs carried in the memories of the folk from one generation to another and sung in public or private, usually among country people. The second class, the broadside ballads, consists of journalistic verse narratives composed and printed for sale at a penny or so and hawked about the streets of London and elsewhere by balladmongers and peddlers. Although they are not so well known to the general reader as the folk ballads, the broadsides were produced in enormous quantities, were well known to the people, and often became traditional songs. The third class comprises the literary ballads or ballads of art, which this book treats. These are the product and possession not of the common people of village or city but of sophisticated poets writing for literate audiences. They are printed poems rather than songs, and they have no traditional life. Despite great variations among individual examples, the literary ballads as a class are conscious and deliberate imitations of folk and broadside ballads.

It would be hard to find another specialized poetic type which had been so frequently produced by so many poets of diverse kinds as the literary ballad. Not only has the genre been in existence for at least four centuries, but it has assumed a role of considerable importance since the beginning of the Romantic period. Nearly every anthology of the British poetry published since 1798 contains numerous examples of literary balladry. Yet the genre has usually been either ignored by scholars or treated only indirectly in studies of individual poets. The most helpful, albeit too brief, discussions have been those written by students of folk and broadside balladry, whose special knowledge has enabled them to speak authoritatively of the whole ballad field.

I have based this study on the frequently tested assumption that readers, teachers, and critics of English poetry usually have too sketchy a knowledge of ballad backgrounds to fully appreciate literary balladry. And I have further assumed that the relationships between the ballads of the people and the ballads of art must be made clear before a meaningful analysis of the latter can be achieved. This study is designed both to increase the reader's enjoyment of literary balladry and to provide the information about its origins which is necessary to sound critical judgment. Much emphasis is placed on acquainting the reader with the various kinds of folk and broadside ballads which the poets have imitated. Because both the literary ballads and the models upon which they are based are so widely scattered, it has also seemed helpful to include some information about the location and extent of this material. And because the historians of literature have had little to say about the ballads of art, I have tried to indicate their importance in the relatively recent history of English poetry. Finally, I have sought to call attention to that artistry by which the skilled poet rises above his materials of imitation and transmutes mere verse into poetry.

G. Malcolm Laws, Jr.

Philadelphia, Pennsylvania
October 1971

1

Literary Ballad Styles

IN the field of balladry, definition by example has often
been found more enlightening than abstract verbalizing.
Thus one may begin by identifying as literary ballads such
frequently anthologized poems as the following: Wordsworth's
"Lucy Gray," Scott's "The Eve of St. John," Southey's "The
Battle of Blenheim," Tennyson's "The Charge of the Light
Brigade," Rossetti's "Sister Helen," Housman's "Is My Team
Ploughing?" Hardy's "Ah, Are You Digging on My Grave?"
and Yeats's "The Ballad of Father Gilligan." While these
pieces display many differences, they also have enough in
common to justify their inclusion in a single literary genre.
Each of them is a dramatic narrative and thus displays the
one basic and unvarying characteristic of all the pieces
covered by this study. In each poem the story is presented in
a series of short, rhymed stanzas and, on the whole, in simple,
straightforward language. But most important, each poem
owes its form and style and its very existence to the great
ballad tradition which has flourished in the British Isles for
several hundred years.

As I have indicated in the Foreword, the great mass of
subliterary British balladry is somewhat arbitrarily divided into

popular or traditional balladry (balladry of the folk) and
~~broadside or street balladry~~ (balladry of the printing press).
The former type dates from the late Middle Ages, though
most of the better-known ballads were probably composed in
the sixteenth and seventeenth centuries. The latter type, by
definition, had to await the practice of printing, but its an-
cestors are to be found among the short verse chronicles of the
earlier period. Broadside balladry flourished from the early
sixteenth century to the late nineteenth. Many of the later
pieces which originated as broadside ballads entered tradition
to take their place in great numbers beside the older popular
ballads and frequently to supplant them. To confuse matters
further, many of the popular ballads made the journey in
reverse and were printed as broadsides. Both types exist,
often side by side, in manuscripts, in printed collections, and
in the repertories of folk singers. Despite the overlapping and
frequent merging of the two types, it is still convenient to
keep them separate for purposes of discussion.

No estimate of the number of ballads of folk and broadside
types composed and circulated during the past four hundred
years can be made with certainty, but thousands of different
ballads in tens of thousands of texts have been preserved in
manuscript and print and have been collected in the field
from traditional singers. The disappearance of balladry, which
all collectors since the days of Walter Scott have feared, has
yet to occur. Folk ballads and those of broadside origin are
very much alive in tradition throughout the English-speaking
world.[1]

Hardly a British poet since the days of the first Elizabeth
can have been unfamiliar with balladry. If he was a city man,
the poet would hear romantic or sensational broadsides sung
or recited in the streets and would see them offered for sale
in stalls or stationers' shops. In the mid-nineteenth century, as
Thackeray and others have reported, the ballad sheets were
displayed in rows hanging from strings tied to a wall or fence.

If the poet was a rural Englishman, Scot, or Irishman he would hear ballads in inns and taverns and at fairs and other local gatherings, even if his own household contained no singers. And all poets, at least since the appearance in 1765 of Thomas Percy's *Reliques of Ancient English Poetry*, have been familiar with published ballad collections.

Some understanding of the pervasiveness of balladry in the British Isles is necessary to an understanding of the involvement of poets with the ballad type. I do not mean that all the poets admired balladry. Their attitude often depended on the type of balladry to which they were exposed. The city poet, constantly assailed by cheap broadsides, often scorned the ballad as doggerel worthy only of parody. The country poet, having probably been raised in a tradition of folksong at least part of which had beauty and some poetic merit, was more likely to treat the ballad with respect and regard it as worthy of his best imitative efforts. And those poets who were primarily inspired by the collections of Percy and his many successors often found in the old printed ballads the excitement and glamor of the romantic past. Thus their imitations tended to be archaic in style and substance. The British ballad, then, in one form or another, has been generally familiar to British poets since its inception and has inspired varied responses including imitation, rewriting, parody, condemnation, and praise. The poets, in short, did everything but ignore the ballad. As a result we have a large body of English poetry which could not have existed without the folk and broadside models which are its prototypes.

One can only speculate about the reasons which impel a poet to imitate a type which seems so simple and undemanding as the ballad. Some perhaps felt a little of that contemptuous jealousy with which serious artists regard crude but successful journalists and wanted to show that they could do better. For others, ballad imitation was apparently a youthful romantic enthusiasm to be supplanted by later interests. But most of the literary balladists must have recognized the fact that the ballad form offered an excellent way of telling a short and dramatic story. Then, too, there was a kind of magic about the ballad which produced a direct emotional impact upon people of all levels of literary sophistication. It was an old war ballad that moved Sir Philip Sidney's heart, and many a later poet has recorded the profound impression which balladry made upon him. Here was a challenge, perhaps, to attempt a form which retained its power despite everything the nonpoets could do to it. And balladry was not all bad poetry. Sometimes it achieved near perfection in the happy suiting of the dramatic phrase to the occasion or in the poignant portrayal of tragedy.

Of course the literary balladists discovered that the apparently simple ballad patterns contained a multitude of difficulties, not the least of which, as Wordsworth's critics were quick to point out, was the pitfall of banality. Other problems involved trying to seem original while being frankly imitative, writing in an unnatural idiom, and attempting to produce a real poem rather than a poetic curiosity. That many poets fell into these traps will be apparent in the pages that follow. Fortunately a significant number successfully avoided them.

Since all ballad composition is imitative in that it is based on conventional patterns, it is not always easy to distinguish between literary ballads and ballads composed for folk assimilation or for the broadside press. The anonymity of a piece is sometimes a helpful criterion. That is, the literary balladists tend to make a claim of authorship while the producers of balladry for the people do not. This may seem an odd and arbitrary distinction, but it is a meaningful one. While there was a good deal of ballad composition by established poets prior to 1750, most of it was designed as genuine broadside balladry for popular consumption. There was very little balladry intended for inclusion in the canon of an author's poetical works. Much of what little there was found its way into Percy's *Reliques,* where it exerted some influence on the future course of literary balladry. Thomas Percy's anthology is, in fact, the single most important source of inspiration for the literary balladists of the pre-Romantic and Romantic periods.[2]

Percy's collection, he says on the title page, consists of "Old Heroic Ballads, Songs, and Other Pieces of Our Earlier Poets, together with Some Few of Later Date." Thus the *Reliques* contained rather miscellaneous materials from various sources, including many ballads of folk and broadside origin. The *Reliques* helped make ballad study and ballad imitation both respectable and popular and initiated a series of ballad activities which have continued in the English-speaking world to the present day.

In his choice of styles for imitation, the literary balladist has been limited only by his knowledge of balladry as it came to him from various sources. He was free to select or reject whatever stylistic features he chose, and he could, of course, draw heavily upon other people's literary ballads and upon nonballad sources. The fact that Percy's collection offered the early ballad writer examples of almost all the literary ballad styles which were later to be widely produced, as well as a variety of folk and broadside types, made it the first textbook of many literary balladists. That it led a number of them astray will emerge in the pages that follow.

The typical student of literature has been taught to think of balladry in terms of romantic and archaic pieces like "Sir Patrick Spens," "Edward," "Sweet William's Ghost," and "Lord Thomas and Fair Annet," each of which appears in the *Reliques* with the designation "A Scottish Ballad." From pieces like this he has learned to recognize such features of the traditional ballad as violent and elemental action, the fifth-act beginning of the story, characters of high rank, repeated speech formulas or clichés, and references to gold and silver. But pieces of this type appear in Percy's anthology along with such typical broadsides as "The Children in the Wood," "George Barnwell," "The Blind Beggar's Daughter of Bednall

Green," and "The Spanish Lady's Love." Such ballads are very different in form and substance from the romantic folk ballads. Then, too, Percy included very old ballads from manuscripts which long antedated the folio manuscript which inspired him to build his collection. Two such ballads are "The Ancient Ballad of Chevy Chase" (otherwise "The Hunting of the Cheviot") and "The Battle of Otterburne," which, coming as they do from fifteenth-century manuscripts, would seem especially deserving of the title term "ancient." Other pieces, like "Little Musgrave and Lady Barnard," "The Bailiff's Daughter of Islington," "Child Waters," and "Barbara Allen's Cruelty," seem clearly of the folk type, though they do not have the added flavor of the Scottish dialect forms. Other kinds of poems in the *Reliques,* including half a dozen "mad songs" and various Elizabethan lyrics, do not concern us here.

Despite the variety of his collection, Percy was not satisfied to present his materials as he found them but felt called upon to revise, correct, and amend in such a wholesale way that one can never be sure of the authenticity of a text. This tampering was not limited to improvements in diction and meter but extended to the creation of numerous whole stanzas in a style considered suitable to the rest of the work. The most flagrant example of this kind involves "The Child of Elle," a fragment which Percy admitted having completed. What he did not say was that the thirty-nine lines of the fragment had become no fewer than two hundred under his treatment. While he tried to keep to the spirit and phrasing of his originals, Percy's contributions tended toward wordiness and sentimentality, weaknesses more typical of the broadsides than of the folk ballads.

If Percy's editorial practices seem reprehensible from a scholarly point of view, it may be said in his partial defense that almost all editors of ballad collections for the general public have yielded to the temptation to complete and correct their texts as well as to produce composite texts from two or more originals. The second great ballad editor, Sir Walter Scott, whose *Minstrelsy of the Scottish Border* appeared in two volumes in 1802 and in three volumes in 1803, was like Percy a great improver of texts and was not above passing off as traditional his own partial or complete compositions. It was not until Professor Francis J. Child's monumental compilation, *The English and Scottish Popular Ballads* (Boston, 1882–98) appeared that the reader could be sure that the editor was applying the strictest scholarly standards to his received texts. But by that time so much damage had been done by earlier editors that the results of their tampering are still enshrined in the Child collection.

Considering that various editors since Child have reverted to some of the questionable practices of Percy and Scott, it is safe to say that the literary balladists have been to some degree dependent upon the taste of editors who have selected certain ballads from the large number available and who have exercised considerable control over the style and substance of their texts. For one thing it seems probable that the metrical and verbal polish of most literary ballads is attributable in part to the fact that the anthologists have usually avoided the corruptions of folk tradition and of the broadside press and have presented texts of exceptional smoothness and completeness.

Percy included in the *Reliques* ballads from various sources including old broadside sheets, but apparently he did not regard the ballad sheets being sold in the London of his own day as sufficiently respectable sources for inclusion, nor did he investigate ballads current in oral tradition. Perhaps he would have been surprised to learn that many of his archaic English and Scottish folk ballads and English broadsides enjoyed an active traditional life in the eighteenth century. He certainly could not have foreseen that the popularity of some of them would continue into the twentieth.

Scott's great collection, to which he and his friends contributed a number of literary ballads, was based largely upon

traditional texts from the border country. Thus the *Minstrelsy*
has a kind of integrity and consistency which Percy's book
lacks, though it is of necessity less varied and catholic in its
subject matter than the earlier collection. The imitator of the
Border Minstrelsy would lean naturally toward the Scottish
folk manner. But the literary balladists were by no means
limited to the collections of Percy and Scott. Numerous ballad
collections appeared late in the eighteenth century and
throughout the nineteenth, including David Herd's *Ancient
and Modern Scottish Songs* (1776), Thomas Evans's *Old Bal-
lads, Historical and Narrative* (1784), Joseph Ritson's *Pieces
of Ancient Popular Poetry* (1791), and William Motherwell's
Minstrelsy, Ancient and Modern (1827). The numerous bal-
lad collections were supplemented by many kinds of antholo-
gies and songbooks as well as by the always available products
of the prolific ballad press. The amount and diversity of this
material is remarkable.[3]

In general the poets have not had scholarly or folkloristic
interests in the ballad, nor have they thought of balladry in
terms of song. They have been influenced largely by edited
and printed texts of varying ages, types, and degrees of authen-
ticity. The diversity of the styles, stanzaic patterns and subjects
of literary balladry is traceable with few exceptions to the
diversity of the source materials in folk and broadside balladry
and occasionally in earlier literary balladry. The average reader
of English poetry, whose acquaintance with balladry is largely
limited to a few of the Child pieces, would naturally be unable
to place most literary ballads within any meaningful frame of
reference. But an eighteenth- or nineteenth-century reader of
the ballad collections, who would also be acquainted with the
balladry of the journals and of the streets, would at once
recognize attempts to imitate familiar ballad patterns.

No problem in ballad study is more persistent or resistant
than that of trying to produce satisfactory and meaningful
classifications for a great mass of diverse material. One ap-

proach is to consider the style of the pieces, which tends to vary according to the age of the text, its immediate source, its ultimate source, its editorial treatment, and its region of origin. To begin with the broadest and most useful of stylistic distinctions, we may draw a dividing line between the romantic and archaic folk ballad, usually from Scottish tradition, and the printed contemporary broadside. These two styles dominate both the balladry of the people and that of the poets. For convenience, these will be referred to from here on as folk ballad and broadside ballad style.

Traditional folk ballad style, which is highly distinctive, is to be found in many of the best of the Child ballads. It is observable, for example, in "Child Maurice" (Child no. 83), a gruesome story of jealousy and mistaken identity. In the text of the Scottish collector William Motherwell, a young man, Child Noryce, whose horse is shod with silver and gold, asks his servant to take a glove to Lady Barnard with the request that she meet him secretly in the greenwood. When the youth hesitates, his master speaks sharply:

> "O do I not give you your meat," he says,
> "And do I not pay your fee?
> How dare you stop my errand?" he says;
> "My orders you must obey."

The boy goes to the castle and delivers the message but is overheard by Lord Barnard, who says to himself:

> "O little did I think there was a lord in the world
> My lady loved but me!"

He disguises himself in women's clothes, goes to the wood, and confronts Child Noryce, who realizes too late that he has been tricked. The last five of the eighteen stanzas follow:

> Lord Barnard he has a little small sword,
> Hung low down by his knee;

He cut the head off Child Noryce,
  And put the body on a tree.

And when he came to his castell,
  And to his ladie's hall,
He threw the head into her lap,
  Saying, "Lady, there's a ball!"

She turned up the bloody head,
  She kissed it frae cheek to chin
"Far better do I love this bloody head
  Than all my royal kin.

"When I was in my father's castel
  In my virginity,
There came a lord into the North,
  Gat Child Noryce with me."

"O wae be to thee, Lady Margaret," he said,
  "An ill death may you die;
For if you had told me he was your son,
  He should ne'er have been slain by me." [4]

This text, having come directly from tradition, shows considerable metrical irregularity and some other signs of wear, but it tells its story with folk-ballad vigor, impersonality, and lack of moralizing. It contains various clichés, such as the reference to meat and fee, the "little small sword," the kissing "frae cheek to chin," and the curse "an ill death may you die." The story is dramatized, largely by means of dialogue, rather than summarized. Its understatement of emotion becomes especially powerful when connected with violent action and death. And the tale is so compressed that its few stanzas contain the plot of a novel or play. This particular ballad, though not this text, did in fact become the basis of John Home's tragedy *Douglas* (1756). Finally, the language of the ballad is simple, direct, and passionate. It is easy to see how such a piece could fix itself in the folk memory.

One does not have to look far among the literary ballads before encountering pieces using essentially the same style and stanza pattern. The following stanzas from Rosetti's "Stratton Water" are an example:

> "O many's the sweet word, Lord Sands,
>   You've spoken oft to me;
> But all that I have from you today
>   Is the rain on my body.
>
> "And many's the good gift, Lord Sands,
>   You've promised oft to me;
> But the gift of yours I keep today
>   Is the babe in my body." [5]

Even in this brief excerpt one can observe a character of high rank, a situation of passion, the liberal use of dialogue and incremental repetition, and the familiar ballad meter with its *a b c b* rhyme.

Here is folk style from a ballad by Sir Walter Scott:

> The Warden's daughters in Lochwood sate,
>   Were all both fair and gay,
> All save the Lady Margaret,
>   And she was wan and wae.
>
> The sister Jean had a full fair skin,
>   And Grace was bauld and braw;
> But the leal-fast heart her breast within
>   It weel was worth them 'a. [6]

One soon comes to recognize and respond to the peculiar flavor of this kind of stanza and to admire it for its charm, perhaps beyond its deserving. Swinburne captures just the right note of magic in the old ballad phrasing:

> "O wha will get me wheaten bread
>   And wha will get me wine?

> And wha will build me a gold cradle
> To rock this child of mine?
>
> . . . .
>
> "Nae silk maun come upon my feet,
> Nae gowd into my hair;
> My brothers smite me on the mouth,
> Where nae man shall kiss mair." [7]

And a twentieth-century Irish poet, Padraic Gregory, comes even closer to traditional style in his imitation of the Scottish ballad idiom:

> "There's saut tears in your eyen, mither,
> Your eyen but an' your cheek,
> An' why dae ye channer sair, mither,
> An' why will ye na speak?"
>
> "Ye'll ne'er set foot o' a ship, Ronald,
> O' teak-wood or o' aik,
> An' ye'll na ken, this side the grave,
> The ease o' your heart's love-ache." [8]

Actually there is far more variation in the style of the traditional folk ballads and their imitations than these few rather similar examples would indicate, but we are now concerned only with the broadest general distinctions. The stanzas quoted might be said to represent a distillation of those qualities which give the northern English or Lowland Scots ballad its distinctive flavor: poetic and emotional intensity, elemental action, and conventionalized language, often archaic and dialectal. The literary ballads based on this pattern vary little from one age to another. In all these examples the poet consciously gives an archaic flavor to his poem by his choice of incident, setting, and phraseology.

Where the literary ballads have been based on broadside models, stylistic identification is not so clear-cut. For one thing, the broadside versifiers used the language of uneducated speech, somewhat distorted by the demands of rhyme and meter. Furthermore they frequently adopted the journalistic jargon of the age, which offered a convenient though unpoetic substitute for original phrasing. Thus broadside style tends to vary noticeably from one age to another, while folk-ballad style, being traditional, tends to reject innovation. Consequently it is still possible to distinguish meaningfully between the style of the broadside press and that of the folk.

What we call the printed broadside style has so few distinctive verbal qualities that at times it seems to be no style at all. To some extent it may be described in terms opposite to those applied to folk balladry. It is realistic rather than romantic, contemporary rather than remote or timeless; it deals with the common man rather than with people of high rank; it is moralistic and subjective rather than detached; its clichés are used to fill out the stanza rather than to advance the story; it is likely to be too detailed, and yet it tends to summarize rather than dramatize; and what is perhaps most objectionable from a literary point of view, its language is often flat and nonpoetic. Yet the broadside ballad was extremely popular among the uneducated because it catered to that widespread interest in the newsworthy and sensational which has been the mainstay of many newspapers and magazines. And it always told its story in a clear and straightforward manner which everyone could understand.

That famous old ballad "The Children in the Wood" will serve to illustrate some of these differences between folk and broadside style. After nine stanzas detailing the death of the children's parents and the terms of their father's will, which leaves everything to their guardian, an uncle, if the children should die, the ballad reports the uncle's actions as follows:

> He bargain'd with two ruffians strong,
> Which were of furious mood,
> That they should take these children young,
> And slaye them in a wood:
> He told his wife an artful tale,

> He would the children send
> To be brought up in fair London,
> With one that was his friend.
>
> Away then went these pretty babes
> Rejoycing at that tide,
> Rejoycing with a merry minde,
> They should on cock-horse ride.
> They prate and prattle pleasantly,
> As they rode on the waye,
> To those that should their butchers be,
> And work their lives decaye.

The two succeeding stanzas describe the sudden remorse of one of the ruffians and his killing of the other when he insists on completing the bargain. The ballad then proceeds:

> He took the children by the hand,
> Tears standing in their eye,
> And bad them straitwaye follow him,
> And look they did not crye:
> And two long miles he ledd them on,
> While they for food complaine:
> Staye here, quoth he, I'll bring you bread,
> When I come back again.
>
> Those pretty babes, with hand in hand,
> Went wandering up and downe;
> But nevermore could see the man
> Approaching from the town:
> Their pretty lippes with black-berries,
> Were all besmear'd and dyed,
> And when they sawe the darksome night,
> They sat them downe and cryed.[9]

The ballad continues for five more stanzas detailing the death of the children and the calamities which befall their uncle as a result of his wickedness.

While I feel confident in assuming a certain kind of emotional response to the text of "Child Maurice," I am uncertain about pieces like "The Children in the Wood." Clearly it displays most of the faults characteristic of broadside style, and the verse rarely rises above the level of doggerel. And yet the ballad somehow survives all that can be said against it. It was this ballad, in fact, which Addison praised in the *Spectator*,[10] and it is this which Wordsworth used to defend his own poetic practices in the Preface to *Lyrical Ballads*. Perhaps the ballad's air of sincere conviction and truth captures one's sympathy and overcomes one's judgment. The story is certainly more believable than that of "Child Maurice." If we admire the poetic imagination of the author or reviser of the folk ballad, we may say that "The Children in the Wood" displays no poetic imagination at all. But it does offer an honest depiction of a wide range of human emotions and behavior and it tells an unforgettable story. This is a claim which can be made for surprisingly few works of literature.

Of course "The Children in the Wood" is of such antiquity —it was entered in the *Stationers' Register* in 1595—has been so firmly established in tradition, and has been so frequently reprinted that it may be regarded as an aristocrat of broadsides. Less well known pieces would display the faults of the typical broadside to a greater degree.

"George Barnwell," which Percy calls a seventeenth-century ballad, recites the events leading to the downfall of an apprentice who is incited to robbery and murder by the wiles of a harlot. It belongs to a class of broadsides sometimes called "goodnights" in which penitent felons, just before their execution, bid farewell to their friends and warn others against lives of crime. From beginning to end this ballad of ninety-one stanzas displays such broadside characteristics as tedious circumstantial detail, forced rhyming, and flat diction. It starts like this:

> All youths of fair England
> That dwell both far and near,

Regard my story that I tell,
  And to my song give ear.

A London lad I was.
  A merchant's prentice bound;
My name George Barnwell; that did spend
  My master many a pound.

Take heed of harlots then,
  And their enticing trains;
For by that means I have been brought
  To hang alive in chains.[11]

In "The Last of the Flock," one of Wordsworth's contributions to *Lyrical Ballads,* the poet makes use of the conventional phrasing and confessional tone of a "goodnight" in telling a story of very different kind. Such a stanza as the following, which wavers on the brink of doggerel, clearly displays the broadside manner:

To wicked deeds I was inclined,
And wicked fancies cross'd my mind;
And every man I chanced to see,
I thought he knew some ill of me.
No peace, no comfort could I find,
No ease, within doors or without,
And crazily, and wearily,
I went my work about.
Oft-times I thought to run away;
For me it was a woeful day.[12]

A century after Wordsworth's poem was first printed, A. E. Housman made still another use of the goodnight in commenting ironically upon the life and death of Jesus of Nazareth. Probably most of Housman's readers have been unaware of the relationship between "The Carpenter's Son" and broadside balladry. Notice how the poet captures just the right tone of remorse as he retells the old story:

> "Here the hangman stops his cart:
> Now the best of friends must part.
> Fare you well, for ill fare I:
> Live, lads, and I will die.
>
> "Oh, at home had I but stayed
> 'Prenticed to my father's trade,
> Had I stuck to plane and adze,
> I had not been lost, my lads.
>
> "Then I might have built perhaps
> Gallows-trees for other chaps,
> Never dangled on my own,
> Had I but left ill alone." [13]

The serious use of broadside style gave way later in the Romantic period to imitations of the older folk balladry and was out of fashion until Hardy and Housman reinstituted it. In the meantime the broadsides continued to be a source of inspiration to those literary balladists who leaned toward humor and parody.

No one seemed to derive more pleasure from imitating the tedious and illiterate broadside style than Thackeray. Of course, the kind of humor which depends on bad spelling and malapropisms is not popular today, but the Victorian reveled in it. Even in his titles, Thackeray satirized street ballad style, as in "A Woeful New Ballad of the Protestant Conspiracy to Take the Pope's Life." The first stanza is a perfect parody of the Anglo-Irish broadside type known as the "come-all-ye":

> Come all ye Christian people, unto my tale give ear,
> 'Tis about a base consperracy, as quickly shall appear;
> 'Twill make your hair to bristle up, and your eyes to start
> and glow
> When of this dread consperracy you honest folks shall
> know. [14]

(The alleged Protestant plot was to have the pope decapitated by his barber.) Thackeray's stanza may be compared with one from an actual Anglo-Irish broadside, "A New Song on the American War":

> Come all you tender Christians with patience lend an ear,
> And listen to those feeling lines that I have written here,
> I'm sure each eye will shed a tear, if you attention pay,
> While thinking on your loving friends that's in America.[15]

In addition to the broad influences of folk style and contemporary broadside style, the reader of literary ballads will notice that many pieces seem to have followed models different from those already described. A number of eighteenth- and nineteenth-century poets used extreme forms of archaic spelling in an effort to recapture the flavor of the remote past. In doing so they tend to imitate those minstrel ballads or ancient pieces of the broadside type which Percy had resurrected from old manuscripts and had reprinted without orthographic modernization. The first poem in the *Reliques*, "The Ancient Ballad of Chevy Chase," begins as follows:

> The Perse owt of Northombarlande.
>   And a vowe to God mayd he,
> That he wolde hunte in the mountayns
>   Off Chyviat within dayes thre,
> In the mauger of doughte Dogles,
>   And all that ever with him be.[16]

Percy's second piece, "The Battle of Otterbourne," starts like this:

> Yt felle abowght the Lamasse tyde,
>   Whan husbonds wynn ther haye,
> The dowghtye Dowglasse bowynd hym to ryde,
>   In Ynglond to take a praye.[17]

Poor Thomas Chatterton was neither the first nor the last poet to yield to the temptation of passing off as a genuine old ballad one or more of his own compositions. Chatterton's "The Bristowe Tragedy," a ballad of nearly one hundred stanzas, shows the extremes to which a poet might go in imitating antique spelling and phrasing:

> Butt whenne hee came, hys children twaine,
>   And eke hys lovynge wyfe,
> Wythe brinie tears dydd wett the floore,
>   For goode Syr Charleses lyfe.[18]

Actually Chatterton's poem was a pretty transparent fabrication and was easy enough to understand. Others, though they may not have seemed genuinely old, presented the reader with more difficulties. William Motherwell, for example, had a penchant for archaisms and Scotticisms which make some of his literary ballads almost unreadable. "Elfinland Wud," which he calls "an imitation of the ancient Scottish romantic ballad," has two lyrical verses to each stanza and two refrains. Here is a sample:

> Elfinland wud is dern and dreir,
>   (Merrie is the grai gowkis sang,)
> But ilk ane leafis quhyt as silver cleir,
>   (Licht makis schoirt the road swa lang.) [19]

And the poem has twenty-eight more such stanzas. Unless one is trying to deceive a reader, there seems little excuse for this sort of thing.

We have seen examples of literary balladry in archaic folk style (Rossetti, Scott, Swinburne, Gregory), of archaic broadside and minstrel style (Chatterton, Motherwell), and of contemporary broadside style (Wordsworth, Thackeray, Housman). Contemporary folk style without dialectal distinction may be seen in such traditional pieces reprinted by Percy as the English version of "Barbara Allen's Cruelty":

> All in the merrye month of may,
>   When greene buds they were swellin,
> Yong Jemmye Grove on his death-bed lay,
>   For love of Barbara Allen.

. . . .

As she was walking ore the fields,
    She heard the bell a knellin,
And every stroke did seem to saye,
    Unworthy Barbara Allen.[20]

Charles Kingsley's "A New Forest Ballad," a tragic story of
a gamekeeper, his daughter, and the young poacher she loves,
belongs in this category:

Her true love shot a mighty hart
    Among the standing rye,
When on him leapt that keeper old
    From the fern where he did lie.

After a bitter struggle the young man stabs the old one and
then:

The old man drove his gunstock down
    Upon the young man's head;
And side by side, by the water brown,
    These yeomen twain lay dead.

They dug their graves in Lyndhurst yard;
    They dug them side by side;
Two yeomen lie there, and a maiden fair
    A widow and never a bride.[21]

Another example of contemporary folk style may be seen in
Housman's "Farewell to Barn and Stack and Tree," which is
reprinted in full in chapter 4.

Some authors of literary ballads seem to have been in-
fluenced less by folk and broadside style than by the style of
other literary balladists and conventional poets. Their pieces
often appeared in the early and middle eighteenth century
when elegance of expression and delicacy of sentiment took
precedence over the idioms of balladry. Some poets would
combine an obviously literary style with ballad matter. Once
this practice was started, it had a long-range influence. Dr.

John Leyden's "The Mermaid," which his friend Scott
printed in the *Minstrelsy*, belongs in this class. Here are two
typical stanzas:

> That sea-maid's form, of pearly light,
>   Was whiter than the downy spray,
> And round her bosom, heaving bright,
>   Her glossy, yellow ringlets play.
>
> Borne on a foamy-crested wave,
>   She reached amain the bounding prow,
> Then, clasping fast the Chieftain brave,
>   She, plunging, sought the deep below.[22]

Neither the folk nor the readers of broadsides would know
what to make of this language, which is a curious example of
eighteenth-century poetic diction. While later literary ballad-
ists would not, of course, imitate the style of such a piece, they
would perhaps feel free to use nonballad idiom. Some such
explanation may account for the style of "Lord Ullin's Daugh-
ter," a literary ballad by another Scottish poet, Thomas Camp-
bell. Campbell's subject matter, the conflict among a father,
his daughter, and her unwelcome suitor is familiar enough in
balladry, but the diction of this piece is of the sentimental
parlor variety:

> And still they row'd amidst the roar
>   Of waters fast prevailing;
> Lord Ullin reach'd that fatal shore,
>   His wrath was changed to wailing. —
>
> For sore dismay'd, through storm and shade,
>   His child he did discover; —
> One lovely hand she stretch'd for aid,
>   And one was round her lover.[23]

The accompanying diagram, Chart A, indicates in part the
styles of texts available to the literary balladist for imitation.
The circle covers in simplified form the whole range of folk

and broadside balladry. Each of the four styles could, of course, be divided into various subcategories. The term *archaic*, for example, may refer either to old-fashioned matter in a ballad of fairly recent composition or to a truly old relic recovered from an ancient manuscript. Even the terms *folk* and *broadside* are of only limited accuracy, since considerable overlapping occurs in these categories. Thus while minstrel ballads like "Chevy Chase" and "The Battle of Otterbourne" are usually classified, following Child, among the popular or folk ballads, they might with more propriety be regarded as ancestors of the broadsides. More important than pigeonholing individual poems is recognizing the fact that all subliterary balladry may be regarded as a circular continuum in which one kind of ballad shares qualities with the kinds on either side and merges imperceptibly into it.[24]

CHART A

Ballad Styles Reflected in Literary Balladry

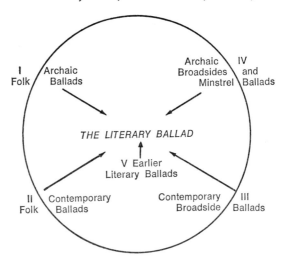

2

Literary Ballad Subjects

ASIDE from the fact that the literary balladist imitates the style of some general class of ballads as indicated on Chart A in chapter 1, he must obviously limit himself further by subject. The most convenient way to give an overall picture of literary balladry is to classify it according to various types of story matter. This procedure may be objected to because it sometimes forces together pieces widely different in origin, style, and intention. Furthermore, any group of subject categories small enough to work with comfortably will result in considerable overlapping of types. Despite the validity of such objections, the method of classifying by subject matter is widely used in ballad study and is probably more helpful than any other.

Although Professor Child decided against indicating ballad types in the definitive edition of his great anthology, he had done so earlier in the popular edition, which was first published in 1857. There he divided all popular ballads into eight large sections or books, which he described as follows: 1) ballads involving superstitions (i.e., the supernatural), 2) tragic love ballads, 3) other tragic ballads, 4) love ballads not tragic, 5) ballads of Robin Hood, 6) ballads of other outlaws and of border forays, 7) historical ballads, and 8) miscellaneous pieces, especially humorous.

When I had occasion to classify the British broadside ballads in American tradition, I found that love was the most popular subject and used four of my eight categories for it. Others dealt with war, the sea, crime, and humor, the last, as in Child, the miscellaneous class. In this connection, an article published half a century ago by R. S. Forsythe is pertinent.[1] After mentioning a handful of pre-Percy imitations, Mr. Forsythe lists the following eight types of literary ballads with numerous examples of each:

1. Imitations of the Plots of Specific Ballads (Percy's "The Child of Elle")

2. Imitations of the Tone and Temper of the Border Ballads (Scott's "Christie's Will")

3. Ballads dealing with the Supernatural or Weird (Southey's "The Old Woman of Berkeley")

4. Ballads based on History or Tradition (Aytoun's "The Heart of the Bruce")

5. Ballads dealing with Religious Subjects (Buchanan's "The Ballad of Mary the Mother")

6. Humorous Ballads (Cowper's "John Gilpin")

7. Ballads founded on Sentiment (Campbell's "Lord Ullin's Daughter")

8. Miscellaneous (Morris's "Two Red Roses Across the Moon")

No student of the ballad is likely to be entirely satisfied with the classifications of other scholars. For my present purposes it is necessary to have categories which can include the Child ballads and the broadsides as well as the literary ballads. Thus I have combined and revised earlier classifications to produce the following main ballad types. (See Chart B). The lower case letter indicates a folk or broadside ballad. (a) Ballads of the Supernatural (b) of Tragedy (c) of Love (d) of Crime and Criminals (e) of Scottish Border Life (f) of War

CHART B

Types of Literary Balladry

BALLAD INFLUENCES

Ballad Classes I–V (from Chart A)

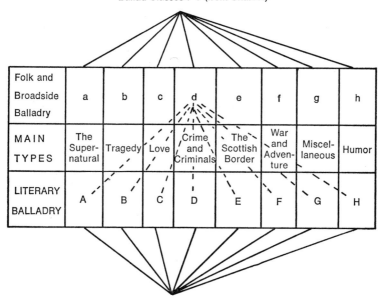

Folk and Broadside Balladry	a	b	c	d	e	f	g	h
MAIN TYPES	The Super-natural	Tragedy	Love	Crime and Criminals	The Scottish Border	War and Adven-ture	Miscel-laneous	Humor
LITERARY BALLADRY	A	B	C	D	E	F	G	H

Folkloristic, Literary, Historical and Other Influences

NON-BALLAD INFLUENCES

Note: The broken lines radiating from "d" indicate that a folk or broadside ballad of any one type may influence a literary ballad of any other.

and Adventure (g) of Miscellaneous Subjects, and (h) of Humor. These same designations, preceded by capital letters can then be used to identify the literary ballads, which are usually descended from folk and broadside ballads of similar type. Chart B is designed to show these relationships and to suggest various other influences on the literary ballad.

As Chart B indicates, the literary balladist will normally imitate the subliterary ballad type closest in style and substance to the kind of story he wants to tell. Thus a literary ballad of the supernatural is likely to display characteristics already observable in supernatural folk or broadside balladry rather than in the balladry of another main type. But occasionally the poet will derive his inspiration from more than one ballad source or subject type or will go entirely outside the realm of balladry for some of his story matter. Thus a literary ballad may display influences from other branches of folklore, from sophisticated literature, from history, or from current events.

BALLADS OF THE SUPERNATURAL (A)

A surprisingly large number of literary ballads tell stories of the supernatural. This fact does not, of course, imply belief on the part of the sophisticated authors in the phenomena related. Whether or not the authors of the traditional ballads of the supernatural believed their stories would be difficult to determine. That the folk who preserved the ballads about ghosts, fiends, witches, and revenants accepted them as literally true is abundantly clear. Those who have collected balladry from traditional singers have been impressed time and again by the fact that the singers wholeheartedly believe the stories they tell in song. Furthermore, if some occurrence in an older ballad ceases to be credible, that ballad is likely to be either dropped from tradition or modified to eliminate the no longer meaningful details. Thus the supernatural has tended to disappear from British traditional balladry in modern times, especially in America, where belief in the supernatural is less strong than in the British Isles. But where belief still exists, the supernatural ballad will be found. The literary balladist may choose the supernatural for a variety of reasons. Perhaps the main one is that the supernatural ballad represents the essence of romanticism and almost automatically confers an antique flavor on the ballad imitation. The supernatural is also useful for psychological purposes in revealing certain aspects of the human mind and personality. And of course any story containing mysterious and dramatic events is likely to have wide appeal.

1. Ballads of Lovers' Ghosts

Of the literary ballads of the supernatural, no subtype has been more popular than that of ghosts, and particularly the ghosts of lovers whose earthly experience was unhappy. It is a truism of ballad ethics that disloyalty in love has dire consequences; these are frequently connected with the appearance of an aggrieved spirit.

A literary ballad which inspired a number of imitations was David Mallet's "William and Margaret." It appears in Percy's *Reliques*, though it had been written forty years before and published more than once. In this ballad the visit of the girl's accusing ghost results in the death of the unfaithful man. Mallet's poem is directly based on two folk ballads, "Fair Margaret and Sweet William" (Child no. 74) and "Sweet William's Ghost" (Child no. 77). Mallet's indebtedness is in fact so great that Professor Child referred to "William and Margaret" simply as the former ballad "rewritten in what used to be called an elegant style." [2]

Matthew Gregory Lewis used a similar theme in his ballad "Alonzo the Brave and the Fair Imogine." Here the note of horror is more pronounced, in keeping with the spirit of his notorious romance *The Monk*, in which the piece first ap-

peared. In this poem, the ghost of Alonzo, with worms eating
it, comes and carries away the faithless girl. "The Fause
Ladye," by Motherwell, which is reprinted in chapter 3, also
belongs here. In it the girl who has stabbed her lover to death
is drowned, slowly and dramatically, by his vengeful ghost. A
gentler story is told in "The Song of the Ghost," by Alfred
Perceval Graves, the father of the contemporary poet. Here
the spirit announces his death, as in "Sweet William's Ghost,"
by a nighttime visit to his beloved. She is found dead of grief
the next day. And in Thomas Moore's "The Lake of the Dis-
mal Swamp" the grieving lover disappears at the lake while
seeking the dead girl, who is said to paddle her canoe there.
The theme of the dead lover who cannot rest seems to appeal
particularly to Irish poets and others who lean toward the
Celtic supernatural.[3]

Rather surprisingly it is a modern poet, Thomas Hardy,
who makes the greatest use of this supernatural motif. In "The
Second Night," for example, the lover meets his girl on a
lonely island and casually apologizes to her for not having kept
his appointment the night before. She speaks complainingly
and then becomes vague to his sight and disappears. It is only
when he returns to his boat that he learns from the oarsman
of her suicide the night before:

> "Yes: found this daybreak, stiff and numb
> On the shore here, whither she'd sped
> To meet her lover last night in the glum,
> And he came not, 'tis said." [4]

In several of Hardy's poems the ghost of an old love ap-
pears to destroy any chance of present happiness. In "The
Pair He Saw Pass," the newly wedded man sees a carriage
containing a bride and groom: the girl he had once intended
to marry and himself. He soon learns that she died at that
hour, and he pines away and soon dies also. Another poem is
a striking dialogue reminiscent of an eighteenth-century broad-

side. A man, in a trance, learns from the ghost of his early love that only he has been true to her memory, although she was another man's wife. He offers to commit suicide and join her, but she explains why he must remain alive:

> "A shade but in its mindful ones
> Has immortality;
> By living, me you keep alive,
> By dying you slay me." [5]

In two poems related to each other in theme, Hardy and Housman use the dead speaker to inquire about the living. Perhaps Hardy recalled the following lines from "The Unquiet Grave" (Child no. 78):

> "Oh who sits weeping on my grave,
> And will not let me sleep?"

His ballad begins:

> "Ah, are you digging on my grave,
> My loved one?—planting rue?" [6]

The dead girl soon learns the answer. Her former love has wed another, and no one, not even the dog who is the second speaker, cares about her anymore. Housman's male ghost in "Is My Team Ploughing?" gets an equally discouraging report including the news that the friend he is questioning has become the lover of the dead youth's girl. In both poems the supernatural is used for ironic commentary on human nature.

2. Ballads of Other Ghosts

The ghosts of literary balladry, like those of folklore, are not bodiless wraiths but are revenants often indistinguishable at first from the living. Those who have died from other than natural causes are especially likely to return. Frequently these are the victims of accident or murder, coming to punish, to comfort, or to accuse. Such beings appear frequently in the folk ballads, less often in the later broadsides.

Kipling's "The Sea-Wife" was obviously inspired by "The
Wife of Usher's Well" (Child no. 79), but it is not a mere
rewriting. The folk ballad tells of three drowned sons who
return home for a brief visit to comfort their grieving mother.
Kipling's sea-wife becomes a kind of prototype of all mothers
who sacrifice sons to the sea, and his poem is in part a hymn
of praise to the seafarers. The folk ballad ends with the cock
crow which calls the ghosts home, but in Kipling's poem the
sailors, both the lucky and the unlucky, are always coming and
going:

> Home, they come home from all the ports,
>   The living and the dead;
> The good wife's sons come home again
>   For her blessings on their head! [7]

A large number of ballads are based on the folk belief that
murder is likely to be exposed or punished by supernatural
means. Allan Cunningham's "The Bonnie Bairns" is a re-
writing of "The Cruel Mother" (Child no. 20), the story of a
woman who murders her illegitimate twins and later attempts
unwittingly to befriend their ghosts. They denounce her and
say that her place is in hell. Cunningham's version is much
kinder—and to that extent less like a typical folk ballad. Noth-
ing is said directly of the murder, although the mother is de-
scribed as having hands "red-wet wi' sin." And here the babies,
who now "live where woe never is," plead in vain to have her
join them. The final stanza follows:

> And O! and O! said thae babes baith,
>   Take her where waters rin,
> And white as the milk of her white breast,
>   Wash her twa hands from sin.[8]

But the motive of revenge is seen in Robert Southey's "Lord
William," in which the ghost of the murdered heir gives a cry
like a child in distress and lures his uncle to death by drown-
ing.

3. *Ballads of Magic Transformations*

A familiar story type in folk and fairy tales as well as in the ballads is that of young people who have been transformed into unattractive creatures by envious stepmothers with powers of witchcraft. Such a folk ballad is "The Laily Worm [Loathly Serpent] and the Machrel [Mackerel] of the Sea" (Child no. 36), in which a boy and a girl are turned into the creatures named in the title. They are rescued only when the "worm" identifies himself to his father and accuses his stepmother of the deed. Her husband has her burned as a witch. Such folk ballads are closely related in subject matter to various medieval romances and may be regarded as partial retellings of the older stories. A related literary ballad is Robert Buchanan's "The Green Gnome." In this a girl riding through the forest is accosted and kissed by an ugly green gnome. She calls upon Christ to protect her, and at the sacred name the gnome is transformed into a handsome young man who will marry the girl. Here Buchanan combines witchcraft and fairy lore in having the youth explain that his stepmother's spell has kept him in fairyland for seven years.

Walter Scott's "Alice Brand," from *The Lady of the Lake,* tells a more complicated story but one soundly based in folklore. Alice and her lover live in the woods as outlaws because he fought and slew her brother on the night of their elopement. An elfin knight, jealous of their presence, sends a hideous dwarf to cast a spell on them. Alice protects them by making the sign of the cross three times, and the dwarf becomes the brother she had thought slain. He says that he was kidnaped by the elves just after the fight. Appropriate as they may be in their settings of romantic legend, such ballads seem little more than versified fairy tales.

Quite different in its sophistication and in its symbolic implications is Andrew Lang's "The Milk-White Doe," which seems related to the traditional ballad of Irish origin called

"Molly Bawn." In Lang's ballad a girl who turns into a doe every ninth midnight is pursued by hunters led by her brother. Finally he gives the doe a fatal wound. In the traditional piece, which does not have overtones of incest, it is the girl's lover who shoots the white swan into which she has been temporarily transformed.

4. *Ballads of Witches and Devils*

Witches may be defined as human females whose trafficking with the devil has given them magic powers. Their presence in traditional balladry is understandable, since belief in witchcraft was for centuries widespread throughout Europe. Not all ballad witches are the old hags one associates with Halloween; some are simply young women who have been crossed in love and are eager to get revenge. Rossetti properly refers to the heroine of his ballad "Sister Helen" as a witch,[9] for burning a waxen model of her former lover and thereby causing his death is an act of witchcraft. And in Swinburne's powerful ballad "The Witch-Mother," jealous anger sends the abandoned mistress to the devil for wicked advice. William Bell Scott, the poet-painter and friend of both Swinburne and Rossetti, combines witchcraft and fairy lore as Buchanan does. In "A Lowland Witch Ballad," the old witch lies in wait for someone else's bridegroom, puts him under a spell, and sends him for a cup of "wisdom-wine." She drinks it and becomes a "radiant damozel," who charms him into disappearing from earth with her.

There is some confusion in Scott's "The Eve of St. John" between the murdered lover as revenant and the devil. Perhaps Scott was thinking of "The Daemon Lover" (Child no. 243), in which the devil in the form of her old lover lures a woman away from her family and drowns her. In the literary ballad, the woman meets the ghost of the lover murdered by her husband and invites him to her bower. Once there he seems to be transformed into the devil as he brands her wrist in a fiery grip. James Hogg's "Mess John" may have been known to Rossetti. It tells of a priest whose unlawful love for a maid leads him to yield to the devil's temptation and make a waxen figure by means of which to torment her by burning and entice her to him. This long and complicated ballad, the author points out, is firmly based in local legend. The freeing of the girl from the priest's power comes about only when he is shot to death by a man brave enough to oppose him with strong Christian magic. Hogg says that the story has some factual basis and that the priest apparently was killed. A story like this has far more sociological and historical interest than one like "The Green Gnome." While stories of witches and devils may seem remote from contemporary experience, they offer some glimpses into the darker recesses of the human soul, and they serve as a reminder that the struggle between good and evil may be portrayed in a variety of ways.

5. Ballads about Other Supernatural Beings

A number of literary ballads deal with the effect upon mortals of meetings with otherworldly creatures. Occasionally such meetings are beneficial; more often they are dangerous or fatal. The most famous folk ballad in this category, and one with a happy ending, is "Thomas Rymer" (Child no. 37), which tells of the Queen of Elfland's taking Thomas on a trip with her and showing him many marvels. She keeps him as her lover in fairyland for seven years and gives him his miraculous poetic or musical powers. Keats's "La Belle Dame Sans Merci" is the best known but least specific reworking of this story. The knight-at-arms has had a harrowing and perhaps fatal experience. Sir Walter Scott presents the tale in three parts in the *Minstrelsy,* the first traditional, the third entirely his own. In it he tells of Thomas's final appearance in Ercildoune, his singing about Tristram and Isolde, and his leaving the earth forever with the hart and hind which have come for him. And Rudyard Kipling built still another ballad on

Thomas's supernatural powers. In "The Last Rhyme of True Thomas," the king comes to dub Thomas a knight and remains to be taught a lesson in humility. Thomas's magical skill as a harper gives the king his first insight into his own life and character. In the last stanza of this fine ballad, Thomas ironically contrasts his power with that of the king:

> "I ha' harpit ye to the throne o' God,
> I ha' harpit your midmost soul in three;
> I ha' harpit ye down to the Hinges o' Hell,
> And—ye—would—make—a knight o' me!" [10]

Many human victims of the love of otherworldly creatures fare far worse than did Thomas the Rhymer. The general idea seems to be that since mortals are not equipped to live in the world of the immortals, death is often the price of such encounters. In James Hogg's "The Mermaid," for example, the beautiful creature of the lake warns the young man against kissing her, but he is unable to resist and dies shortly thereafter. Other stories of dangerous mermaids have been popular with the literary balladists, who have generally built their stories upon beliefs widely current among seafaring people. In "The Mermaid" (Child no. 289), a ship runs aground soon after a mermaid is sighted sitting on a rock and combing her hair. In Richard Garnett's "The Mermaid of Padstow," the creature's enmity is motivated by the fact that she has been shot in mistake for a seal. She causes a violent storm which blocks the harbor with sand so that no ship can ever again move in or out of it.

Among the earliest of these poems is "The Mermaid," which Scott's friend Dr. John Leyden based upon a Gaelic ballad.[11] Macphail, returning by boat to the maid of Colonsay, is captured by a mermaid, who takes him to a cave and asks him to love her. Despite seven months' imprisonment, he remains faithful to his true love and finally persuades the mermaid to take him near home, where he escapes. Another early piece of this type is Allan Cunningham's "The Mermaid of Galloway," which the author at first attempted to pass off as traditional when he contributed it to Cromek's collection.[12] In fifty-seven stanzas of archaic spelling and Scots dialect—which would be rather too much for tradition to handle—he tells the story of young Cowehill. Enticed by the song of the mermaid, he ignores both the warnings of his foot-page and the fact that he is betrothed and goes to kiss her. She casts spells upon him and takes him into the sea. His bride-to-be has a long wait, but eventually he returns, cold of hand and cheek to give his final message:

> "O seek anither bridegroom, Marie,
>   On thae bosom-faulds to sleep;
> My bride is the yellow water lilie,
>   Its leaves my brydal sheet!" [13]

Among the malicious creatures of supernatural balladry we find a rather un-British group of fiends derived largely from German and Scandinavian sources.[14] A recurring theme in these half-foreign horror ballads is that of the coming of death in one form or another to carry away an earthly sinner. The ballad which inspired a long series of imitations and variations was Bürger's "Leonora," which was translated by Scott as "William and Helen" and became, along with a translation of Bürger's "The Wild Huntsman," his first published verse. Leonora or Lenore is so distressed when her William does not return with the other soldiers from a crusade that she questions the mercy of God and wishes she were dead. William appears at midnight to take her on a thousand-mile ride to his narrow bridal bed. As they rush together through the night on his horse, the scenery becomes increasingly death-like, and soon they are walking among tombstones and over graves. William Taylor's translation, which inspired Scott's, proceeds as follows:

His head became a naked skull,
Nor hair nor eyne had hee;
His body grew a skeleton,
Whilome so blythe of blee.

And hollow howlings hung in aire,
And shrekes from vaults arose;
Then knew the mayde she might no more
Her living eyes unclose.[15]

The ballad ends with a warning from a ghostly crew to avoid the impiety of questioning the decrees of heaven. The archaisms, the charnel-house details, and the obtrusive moralizing of this ballad and its relatives are all features borrowed by the British imitators.

Sometimes the usual theme of sin and retribution was almost forgotten by the eager young British poets in their desire to be wildly imaginative and shocking. Good taste was also ignored or at least erratically remembered. The fad of the horror ballad reached its height with the publication of *Tales of Wonder* in 1801. This collection consists almost entirely of old and new literary ballads, including many translations from the German and indirectly from the Scandinavian. Its editor and chief contributor was Matthew Gregory Lewis; other major contributors were Scott, Southey, and Dr. John Leyden. Both Scott and Lewis translated Goethe's "The Erl-King," and Lewis included his text in the anthology. In this a father rides through the night holding his young son, who keeps reporting to him the presence of the Erl-king and his attempts to lure him away. Despite his desperate flight to the castle, the father arrives too late, for the baby is dead in his arms. The note of horror is greatly increased in the British ballads. Lewis's "The Cloud King," Leyden's "The Elfin King," and Scott's "The Fire-King" all appear in *Tales of Wonder*. In the first, the heroine is offered the blood of a damsel to drink and the head of a child to eat. In the second, the knight has this experience:

> With panting breast, as he forward press'd,
>   He trode on a mangled head;
> And the skull did scream, and the voice did seem
>   The voice of his mother dead.[16]

In the third, the hero sees his beloved with "death-swimming eyeballs and blood-clotted hair." Perhaps these examples are enough to show why this kind of horror balladry soon expired, partly from its own excesses and partly because it was parodied to death.[17]

6. *Ballads of Miracles*

A final important subtype of supernatural balladry is that which involves religious experiences or legends. This general kind is perhaps already familiar from such pieces as "The Cherry-Tree Carol" (Child no. 54), in which Jesus performs his first miracle from Mary's womb by having the tree bow down to give her fruit. In "St. Stephen and Herod" (Child no. 22), the roasted capon crows *"Christus natus est!"* in confirmation of Stephen's announcement of the Child born in Bethlehem. Another example is "Dives and Lazarus" (Child no. 56). The beggar who is denied meat and drink by the rich man is conducted to heaven by angels when he dies, but the rich man's fate is to be led by serpents to hell. This piece has had understandable appeal among the poor people with whom it is traditional.

Matthew Arnold's only ballad,[18] "St. Brandan," tells of the saint's seeing Judas on an ice floe where he is permitted to cool himself for an hour each year because he was once kind to a leper. A more imaginative story is told in "The Ballad of Judas Iscariot" by Robert Buchanan. The soul of Judas wanders for years bearing his body for which he can find no hiding place. At last he comes to a lighted hall where a feast is about to begin. The Bridegroom causes snowflakes to turn to doves which bear the body away and then invites the soul to enter:

> "The Holy Supper is spread within,
>   And the many candles shine,
>   And I have waited long for thee
>   Before I poured the wine!" [19]

Judas kneels, washes the bridegroom's feet, and dries them with his hair.

The religious ballads include several miracles of the Virgin, the medieval narrative type best known from Chaucer's "The Prioress's Tale." In these Mary appears at a crucial moment to assist someone in his need. Kipling's ballad "Our Lady of the Sackcloth" is, he says, founded on an "Ethiopic version" from a manuscript in the British Museum. An old priest who has always honored the Virgin is relieved of his duties because he can no longer speak clearly. He goes to the desert, where he fasts and prays. As he tries unsuccessfully to make a harsh sackcloth garment, Mary appears and fashions it for him. Later she appears again, this time as a queen of the desert, and gives him a message for his bishop asking that he be restored to duty, and she says to him:

> "For again thou shalt serve at the Offering
>   And thy tongue shall be loosed in praise,
>   And again thou shalt sing unto Mary
>   Who has watched thee all thy days." [20]

A frequently reprinted piece is John Davidson's "A Ballad of a Nun," the story of a passionate doorkeeper of the convent who escapes into the world and returns long afterward to find that the Virgin has assumed her form and kept her place.

Yeats's "The Ballad of Father Gilligan" is well known. Instead of hurrying to the bedside of a dying man, the tired old priest falls asleep in his chair. When eventually he awakes and goes on his mission, he finds that an angel in his shape has been there before him. And in Hardy's "The Lost Pyx: a

Medieval Legend," the priest, having struggled through a storm to the bedside of a dying man, discovers that he has lost the pyx containing the Sacrament. He goes back into the storm and sees a ray of light shining from heaven on a small spot of earth. There is the pyx surrounded by kneeling animals. He returns with it in time for the final rites. Later he marks the place of the miracle with a monument.[21]

7. *Miscellaneous Ballads of the Supernatural*

Of the various supernatural ballads which do not fit easily into any of the previous categories, the most famous is Coleridge's "Rime of the Ancient Mariner." In this extraordinarily complex work of genius, the supernatural is used for religious, philosophical, and psychological purposes, as well as those of art. A couple of ballads dealing with heavenly experiences may be placed here. Rossetti's "The Blessed Damozel" is widely reprinted; Kipling's "Dinah in Heaven" is not. The latter is a cheerful and unsentimental account of a new arrival's successful plea to have his pet dog admitted to heaven by St. Peter. Finally may be mentioned a charming piece by Edwin Muir entitled "The Ballad of the Flood." In this the story of Noah is narrated in the Scottish dialect. Here is a sample stanza:

> But Noah took a plank o' aik,
>   Anither o' the pine,
> And bigged a house for a' his folk
>   To sail upon the brine.[22]

Some reasons for the popularity of the supernatural in literary balladry have already been given. In addition, it may be said that the well-established traditional status of this type makes it appealing to the poets, particularly since it allows so much imaginative latitude. Most literary balladists of the supernatural have resisted the temptation to be merely sensational. In the respectably long history of this type, the desire to shock has been far less prominent than the search for truth.

Having shown how one main ballad type may be divided into a series of subtypes, we may now expand a portion of Chart B. Chart C, which follows, displays the subtypes of supernatural balladry and indicates various ways in which the relationship between the popular and the literary pieces may be diagramed. Most of the titles listed in Chart C have just

CHART C

Sub-Types of Literary Balladry of the Supernatural

SUB-TYPES	Some Type "a" Examples	Some Type "A" Examples
1 Lovers' Ghosts	"Fair Margaret and Sweet William" (Child no. 74)	Mallet: "William and Margaret"
2 Other Ghosts	"The Cruel Mother" (Child no. 20)	Cunningham: "The Bonnie Bairns"
3 Trans-formations	"Molly Bawn" (Laws no. 0 36)ᵃ	Lang: "The Milk-White Doe"
4 Witches and Devils	"The Daemon Lover" (Child no. 243)	Scott: "The Eve of St. John"
5 Other Supernatural Beings	"The Mermaid" (Child no. 289)	Hogg: "The Mermaid"
6 Miracles	"Brown Robyn's Confession" (Child no. 57)	Kipling: "Our Lady of Sackcloth"
7 Miscel-laneous	"Captain Glen" (Laws no. K 22A)	Coleridge: "The Rime of the Ancient Mariner"

from Chart B

a

The Super-natural

A

Legend:

———————▶ A is rewritten from a

— — — — —▶ A is partially based on a

——————— A and a are on the same general subject

— — — — — — A and a have one or more main motifs in common.

• • • • • • • • A and a have one or more sub-motifs in common.

ᵃ See *American Balladry from British Broadsides*.

been mentioned; a word may be said about the others. "Brown Robyn's Confession," like "Our Lady of the Sackcloth," is a miracle of the Virgin. Sinful Robyn, who has been thrown overboard by his mates, is rescued from the sea by Mary and taken to heaven because of his honesty in confessing his heinous crimes. And Captain Glen is like the Ancient Mariner in that his sinfulness brings supernatural retribution. Obviously such a chart as this is only a first step in indicating the relationships between a specific literary ballad and its fore-runners.

BALLADS OF TRAGEDY (B)

The literary ballads of type B may serve as a reminder that basically balladry is the most utilitarian of verse types in that it serves as a vehicle for the effective dissemination of dramatic news. Everyone responds to an exciting story and likes to be assured that it is true. The ballads, both folk and broadside, have served this primary function since their inception. Here we are dealing with the material of predictable and dependable news value, as can be seen by reference to all but the most intellectually oriented of the news media. These, in short, are the stories of tragedy, of murder, accident, and sudden death.

But there is one major difference between the literary ballad of tragedy and the folk or broadside piece as it is received by the people. The reader of the literary ballad can never accept it as having either news value or factual authority; he must respond to it, if at all, as timeless and artistic fiction. And this, of course, is the way many readers have learned to respond to those texts of certain folk ballads which may properly be considered works of art.

Many of the ballads for which we admire the popular genre —pieces like "The Twa Sisters," "The Cruel Brother," "Lord Randal," and "Edward" (Child nos. 10–13) belong in the type of domestic tragedy. The closeness of the family relationship adds greatly to the poignancy and shock of many such ballads. Realizing this, the poets have tried for at least equal success in telling new stories of this kind. This type of ballad has appealed to men whose usual poetic mood is gloomy, like Housman and Hardy, as well as to men of such varied personalities as Swinburne and Kipling.

The simplest of such ballads are touching stories of death and grief. One of these is Wordsworth's "Lucy Gray," the tale of a little girl who wanders to her death in a snowstorm. This is a common broadside ballad type. Housman's "Atys" belongs here too. Waiting eagerly for the return of his son Atys from a hunt, the old king, Croesus, gradually becomes aware that the youth is being carried home dead.

In other ballads death has been caused, often unwittingly, within the family group. Yeats's "The Ballad of Moll Magee" is of this kind. She has been turned away from home by her husband because in her exhaustion she accidentally smothered their baby by lying upon it. And in Hardy's "A Sunday Morning Tragedy," the mother causes her daughter's death by giving her a powerful herb to induce an abortion. Too late she learns that the girl's lover has decided to marry her. This particular kind of realism is different from anything in the romantic folk ballads, though it has parallels in the broadsides.

Not surprisingly, considering the geography of the British Isles, accidental death in the literary ballads most often takes the form of drowning, a subject which in the folk ballads is at least as old as "Sir Patrick Spens" (Child no. 58). In Walter de la Mare's "The Silver Penny" an excursion ends tragically with the death of two children and the sailor who has taken them for a boat ride. In Austin Dobson's "My Landlady," the mother tells of the shadow cast over her life by the drowning of her son many years before. Charles Kingsley's "The Sands of Dee," one of those ballads which everyone knew a few generations ago, tells of Mary who went to call the cattle home and was drowned. As those who reprint this piece sometimes observe, this ballad gave Ruskin an example of the *pathetic fallacy* for his discussion of that term of his own coinage. This is the ballad with the "cruel crawling foam."

One of the most moving and imaginative of these tragic stories is Kipling's "The Gift of the Sea." A young widow whose baby has just died is sharing her grief with her mother. Their emotions stirred and their sense of reality dulled by personal tragedy, the women hear what sounds like a child's cry. They decide that the cry must come from a bird or an animal or even from the baby's soul struggling to free itself. Finally going outside to investigate, the widow finds the body of a newly drowned baby. She returns in anguish to the house:

> And the dead child dripped on her breast,
>   And her own in the shroud lay stark;
> And, "God forgive us, mother," she said,
>   "We let it die in the dark!" [23]

Rossetti's "The White Ship" attempts to recapture a tragic moment in history. It tells of the drowning in 1120 of Prince William, son of Henry I of England, who was lost while trying to save his sister in a shipwreck that took three hundred lives. Still remote in time is Jean Ingelow's "The High Tide on the Coast of Lincolnshire." A warning of danger is given by the mayor when he has the tune "The Brides of Enderby" played on the Boston bells. But the fears of a mother and her son are well founded. The sea wall is down, the land is flooded, and the son has arrived home too late to search for his wife and children. Their bodies are washed to his door the next day.

BALLADS OF LOVE (C)

The proverbial lack of smoothness in the course of true love has long been a fruitful source of ballad subject matter. Of

the vicissitudes faced by lovers none is more familiar in bal-
ladry, more romantic, or inherently more believable than that
of the lovers who face family opposition to their marriage. For
example, more than three dozen such pieces of British broad-
side origin are traditional in America.[24] Numerous others
could be added from among the Child ballads and elsewhere.
Among the oldest literary ballads on this subject is David Mal-
let's "Edwin and Emma," a sentimental eighteenth-century
piece which was long popular. Two virtuous and devoted
lovers are kept apart by the malice of the man's family. He
pines away, and she, hearing his death bell, expires. This is
quite similar in outcome to "Bonny Barbara Allan" (Child
no. 84). But in most such pieces, the action is more violent.
As Professor C. K. Hyder points out,[25] Swinburne's "Earl
Robert" descends from "Willie and Lady Maisry" (Child no.
70), in which the girl's father interrupts their tryst and fatally
wounds her lover. But the phrasing of Swinburne's poem is
largely his own, though his amazing skill with an intensified
ballad idiom makes it seem almost traditional:

> Up then gat her auld father,
> Between the wall and her bed feet;
> "Is there ony breath in your lips, Earl Robert,
> To gar a dead mouth smell sweet?"

And when the deed of murder is done, Annie speaks sadly:

> "O gin ye dig na deep, father,
> I wot ye maun dig wide;
> And set my lord to the nether land,
> And my bairn to the green side." [26]

It was natural for lovers to attempt to escape from parental
tyranny, but they sometimes did so with fatal results. Such a
pair are those in "Lord Ullin's Daughter," by the Scottish
Romantic poet Thomas Campbell. The girl and her Highland
lover are drowned on a stormy night as her father calls his

forgiveness too late to save them. In Swinburne's "The Bride's Tragedy," the girl is rescued from the husband she does not love, but her escape with Willie ends when both are drowned in a raging river.

Not all the love ballads end unhappily. The most frequently retold story in broadside balladry is that of the returned lover, which usually goes like this: Two lovers meet after a long separation. The man, who is in disguise or is not recognized, tests the girl's faithfulness by reporting his own death and observing her reactions. After she has displayed both loyalty and grief, he reveals his identity, and the two have a happy reunion, with marriage in the offing. The popularity in tradition of these naïve stories is one of various indications that successful balladry need not end in violence or tragedy.[27] This was one of the first ballad types imitated in the eighteenth century, probably because such stories were both refined and sentimental. Two once famous pieces are Goldsmith's "The Hermit," which is also called "Edwin and Angelina," and Thomas Percy's "The Friar of Orders Gray." These poems are historically important in helping to make serious ballad imitation respectable, but otherwise they have little to recommend them to modern tastes. In both pieces fickle girls change their minds after scorning their suitors and go searching for them. The once devoted wooers have adopted religious vocations, but the prospect of marriage proves more appealing than the life of hermit or friar, and love triumphs over asceticism.

BALLADS OF CRIME AND CRIMINALS (D)

While there are relatively few literary ballads dealing with crime and criminals, the type has been so well established among the people that it seems worth preserving. In general the criminals of traditional balladry, both folk and broadside, are treated sympathetically if they are not actually regarded as heroes. The major criminal's successful defiance of authority has always had wide appeal. The most obvious and oldest example is, of course, Robin Hood, who owes his very existence to balladry and is the archetype of the outlaw-hero. (The Robin Hood ballads, upon which all prose accounts are built, are nos. 117–54 in Child's collection.) Later and lesser broadside heroes include Dick Turpin in England, Willie Brennan in Ireland, and Jesse James in America.

The outlaw as romantic hero is represented in a quartet of English literary ballads: W. Harrison Ainsworth's "Black Bess," Austin Dobson's "The Ballad of 'Beau Brocade'," and Alfred Noyes's "Dick Turpin's Ride" and "The Highwayman." The last is best known from its frequent appearance in school anthologies. It tells of the landlord's daughter who warns her highwayman lover away from the trap set by the Redcoats by firing the musket which they have tied against her breast. Noyes's other ballad and Ainsworth's deal with Turpin's phenomenal ability to escape capture on his famous mare Black Bess. A two-part ballad, "Dick Turpin's Ride" tells first of a fight in darkness with his captors and his accidental killing of his partner Tom King. The second part dramatizes his escape from London to York on Bess. (Such a ride is the subject of a broadside ballad well established in tradition.) [28] Noyes gives Turpin a troublesome conscience because of the killing, and his Other Self becomes a character in the ballad. Ainsworth's ballad, which has entered tradition by way of a broadside,[29] tells of another fast ride and a cleverly established alibi. Like the others, Dobson's ballad has an eighteenth-century setting. In a long narrative full of good humor and local color, he tells of the chambermaid who goes to warn the stagecoach about the highwayman Beau Brocade and stays to wound and capture him.

Among the hundreds of news stories of criminals which were told on ballad sheets throughout the British Isles during the eighteenth and nineteenth centuries were many whose main object was to capitalize on the bloody and sensational.

But almost invariably such pieces have been quickly forgotten, and the type has not appealed to the literary balladist, who likes characters with whom the readers can identify themselves. Such identification could be achieved in the familiar broadside type known as the "good-night," which has been mentioned in chapter 1. These ballads, which consist of the purported last words of the condemned man before his execution, were composed by the London ballad makers and sold to the printers at a shilling each for distribution on the day of execution and later.[30] The general tone of such pieces tends to be moral and rather sentimental. The criminal regrets his past and warns others against emulating him. Thus he is presented as pitiable rather than heroic. The "good-night" has several descendants and relatives among the literary ballads. Housman's "The Carpenter's Son" has already been quoted.[31] His poem which begins "On moonlit heath and lonesome bank / The sheep beside me graze" is the monologue of a youth who is keeping an all-night vigil for his friend in Shrewsbury jail who will be hanged in the morning. This substitution of an observer for the victim as narrator may be regarded as a variation on the older form. It offers certain advantages in point of view, including that of allowing the narrator to bring his story to its sad conclusion. We find it used again in Kipling's "Danny Deever," where the shock and horror of a fellow soldier's execution are conveyed through the questions of the young recruit and the answers of the sergeant. And Oscar Wilde's "The Ballad of Reading Gaol" falls into this category, too. With tender perception the author captures the feelings of both the condemned man and his fellow convicts.

BALLADS OF THE SCOTTISH BORDER (E)

This category could vary considerably in size depending upon one's interpretation of a border ballad. I am confining it to those pieces in which the special character of border life is emphasized.[32] The literary ballads of this type deal with such subjects as feuds, cattle raids, assaults, and rescues. The life depicted required considerable strength, fortitude, and ingenuity, and these qualities are celebrated in the literary ballads as they are in the folk ballads which inspired them. Because this kind of balladry required specialized knowledge, it is not surprising that it was written largely by border men. The leading practitioners were Walter Scott, his protégé James Hogg, and their friends and followers.

"Jock o' the Side" (Child no. 187) is a good example of a folk ballad of border rescue. Child says of it, "The ballad is one of the best in the world, and enough to make a moss-trooper of any young borderer, had he lacked the impulse." According to Child, John of the Side was an actual border thief of about 1550.[33] The story goes like this: The Laird's Jock, the Laird's Wat, and Hobie Noble go to rescue Jock o' the Side, who has been taken prisoner by the English and lies in Newcastle jail. They go disguised as hucksters, with their horses shod backward to leave a misleading trail. Arriving at the gates of the town, they kill the porter, take his keys, and make their way to Jock, who is bound down in irons. The Laird's Jock takes the prisoner up on his back, and they all escape to the banks of the Tyne, which looks as full as the sea. The Laird's Jock scorns Wat's timidity and helps them all swim across to safety. The story is told in Lowland Scots with great liveliness and good humor. Other ballads, "Archie o' Cawfield" (Child no. 188) and "Kinmont Willie" (Child no. 186), tell very similar stories, the main difference being in the names of the characters and in the preliminary details. The latter piece should perhaps be called a literary ballad because it is under heavy suspicion of being the work of Sir Walter Scott,[34] but since it is not included among his acknowledged poems, I will use other examples.

Scott's "Christie's Will" tells of a border thief who does a favor for the official who once freed him. He kidnaps the judge, Lord Durie, whose decision might go against the official in a lawsuit, and holds him imprisoned until the suit has been won. He then takes the judge back and claims the reward that the king has offered for his return. Scott tells the tale, which is based on fact, in the dialect and in the ballad manner:

> He brought him to the council stairs,
> And there full loudly shouted he,
> "Gie me my guerdon, my sovereign liege,
> And take ye back your auld Durie!" [35]

But what Scott regarded in that piece as rude folk ballad style was not really congenial to him, and his ballads on border subjects tend to depart from ballad simplicity. "The Eve of St. John" makes much more use of local color than would naturally occur in a folk ballad, and the rhyming and metrics frequently show sophistication. "Cadyow Castle," a border minstrel's tale of revenge, makes extreme use of poetic diction:

> "Mid pennon'd spears, a steely grove,
> Proud Murray's plumage floated high;
> Scarce could his trampling charger move,
> So close the minions crowded nigh." [36]

The most enthusiastic, and on the whole most convincing border balladist is James Hogg, the Ettrick Shepherd, whose works are little read today but who in his own times was regarded as one of Scotland's chief poets. A self-educated shepherd who did not learn to read until he was seventeen, Hogg was steeped in the lore of his native border and never treated his material with condescension. He enjoyed turning local history and legends into ballads—an excellent way of insuring the authenticity of the material. The reader may be annoyed by his use of extreme spelling in his imitations of archaic Scots, but the words are usually familiar enough, as in this stanza:

> "O thou hast donne ane manlye deide,
> In bluidye letteris itt muste stande;

> But I'll sett my mark onne thy forheid,
>   And I'll put my mark onne thy rychte hande." [37]

Fortunately he wrote like this only part of the time.

The very titles of Hogg's border ballads give some idea of their substance and flavor: "The Laird of Laristan," "The Fray of Elibank," "Jock Johnstone the Tinkler." In the last named, Johnstone offers to fight with Lord Douglas, who is seeking his love after the Earl of Ross has eloped with her. After Douglas is humiliatingly defeated, the tinker reveals his full identity:

> "Jock Johnstone is my name, 'tis true—
>   But noble hearts are allied to me,
> For I am the Lord of Annandale,
>   And a knight and earl as well as thee." [38]

It is he who has carried off the lady for his brother, the Earl of Ross, to marry, and he has a thousand men to do battle if the need arise. In "The Fray of Elibank" we have the story of Willie Scott of Arden, who with his followers attempts to steal the cattle of Juden (Gideon) Murray of Elibank. The two forces meet in a bloody battle in the Ettrick Forest, and Willie is taken prisoner. He is given the choice of being hanged or marrying Murray's homely but kindly daughter. At first he proudly chooses death, but the sight of his coffin changes his mind, and he and "Muckle-mouth Meg" begin what is to become a happy married life.

These ballads, with their historical backgrounds, their insight into border life and character, and their mixture of violence, pride, and good humor may be considered representative of a noble ballad type.

BALLADS OF WAR AND ADVENTURE (F)

Most of the ballads of the preceding type might with equal logic have been placed here among those of war and adventure. This is simply a much more varied category. It includes ballads of strife and memorable deeds on land and sea, and it deals with events fictional, legendary, and historical. While the ballads of this type may have less to offer the sophisticated reader than those of certain other categories, they are full of meaningful action by people who are appealing in their firm adherence to unwavering moral codes.

1. Ballads of the Sea

From the days of Elizabeth I through at least the first half of the nineteenth century, practically every important sea fight involving the British became a subject of broadside balladry. Most of these poems are forgotten, but they may be seen on the ballad sheets and in the anthologies. Countless other ballads dealt with shipwreck, piracy, fishing, whaling, and other events and occupations of the sea. "The *Golden Vanity*" (Child no. 286) is well known in tradition today, as are the pirate ballads "High Barbary" and "The *Flying Cloud*," the latter largely confined to North American tradition. Ballads about John Paul Jones are known on both sides of the Atlantic.

One of the best of sea narratives is Browning's "Hervé Riel," the story of a Breton sailor who saved the French fleet from the pursuing British in 1692 by piloting it into the harbor of Croisic through the narrow passage which only he could navigate. In form this bears no resemblance to any previous ballad, traditional, broadside, or literary, known to me. The poem has eleven parts varying greatly in line length but held together by tight rhymes and rushing phrases. But in substance and general effect, the poem captures real ballad spirit.[39]

Quite similar in its irregularity, in the rapidity of its movement, and in its rhyming is Tennyson's "The *Revenge*: a Ballad of the Fleet," which attempts to recreate an Elizabethan flavor in its account of Sir Richard Grenville's heroic fight against a far superior Spanish force and his gallant death. It, too, is a powerful poem on a fine ballad subject. That the talents of the two greatest Victorian poets should have shown such similarity in a form of literary balladry, if not elsewhere, is worthy of note.[40] Twenty years earlier Gerald Massey had published a ballad on the same subject entitled "Sir Richard Grenville's Last Fight." It lacks the force and fiber of Tennyson's, but it is more orthodox in form, consisting of tightly rhymed stanzas of seven short lines each.[41]

A sea ballad almost contemporary with the event it recounts is Thomas Campbell's "The Battle of the Baltic," which tells of Nelson's defeating and capturing the Danish fleet. The stanzaic pattern here is unusual but consistent:

> Out spoke the victor then,
> As he hail'd them o'er the wave:
> "Ye are brothers! ye are men!
> And we conquer but to save; —
> So peace instead of death let us bring;
> But yield, proud foe, thy fleet,
> With the crews, at England's feet,
> And make submission meet
> To our king." [42]

Much less romantic is Kipling's "The Ballad of the *Bolivar*," an account of a nightmarish voyage in a leaky cargo ship from which the crew never expects to emerge alive. Here is the chorus:

> *Seven men from all the world back to town again,*
> *Rolling down the Ratcliffe Road drunk and raising Cain:*
> *Seven men from out of Hell. Ain't the owners gay,*
> *'Cause we took the "Bolivar" safe across the Bay?* [43]

The cruel and dangerous life on shipboard is also seen in Masefield's "Cape Horn Gospel–II." This tells of a trip which begins with the captain's killing an impudent sailor, continues with several other deaths, and ends when the ship sinks in a storm. The narrator is on his way home after being rescued and plans to stay there. Ballads like the last two are firmly grounded in tradition. It was long customary for seamen to preserve the events of memorable voyages in ballad form, sometimes as a means of revenge against captains or owners and as a warning to other sailors.[44]

2. Ballads of War

Some of the oldest popular ballad texts, pieces like "The Battle of Otterburn," "The Hunting of the Cheviot (Chevy Chase)," and "The Battle of Harlaw" (Child nos. 161–63) belong in this category as do numerous later accounts of famous engagements. The literary balladists, who have usually been landsmen, have produced more such pieces than those of the sea. This is the only major subtype of literary ballad which relies heavily on historical data. But it is a difficult one to make meaningful to the reader, who generally responds better to the deeds of individuals or small groups than to those of armies, especially if the events happened in the remote past.[45]

The most famous literary ballad of this type in the English-speaking world is, of course, Tennyson's "The Charge of the Light Brigade." The poem was written immediately after the event it celebrates, was widely reprinted, and was even circulated among the troops in the Crimea. Probably no poem has been oftener memorized and declaimed by school children. The hurried trimeter stanzas seem related to those of Michael Drayton's famous ballad "Agincourt," but Tennyson's consist of 8, 9, 9, 12, 11, and 6 lines with no fixed rhyming patter, while Drayton's are regular and rhyme *a a a b c c c b*. Actually Drayton's ballad seems superior in every way and lacks only the journalistic appeal of Tennyson's. The following stanza is typical of the quick movement and high quality which is maintained throughout the older poem:

> This while our noble king,
> His broadsword brandishing,

> Down the French host did ding
>   As to o'erwhelm it;
> And many a deep wound lent.
> His arms with blood besprent,
> And many a cruel dent
>   Bruised his helmet.[46]

The minor Victorian poet George W. Thornbury has a fine ballad, "Culloden," in the same meter. That battle of 1745 so disastrous for the Highland followers of the Stuart cause is dramatized with great power in passages like this:

> Stormy the pipers blew,
> Snow white the ribbons flew,
> Deeper the fury grew,
>   Madder than Flodden,
> Piercing through heart and brain,
> Beating like tempest rain,
> Drove the red hurricane
>   O'er dark Culloden.[47]

Byron goes back to Biblical story for his moving ballad "The Destruction of Sennacherib," the galloping anapests of which effectively introduce the Assyrian horsemen. But Robert Buchanan, like Thornbury, stays on British soil with "The Battle of Drumliemoor," which dramatizes a bloody encounter between the Scottish Covenanters and the king's troopers. Again the stanza, with its alternating hexameter and pentameter lines, is atypical of balladry. And Macaulay's "The Battle of Naseby," a diatribe against the king's forces by a rabid Puritan follower of Cromwell, is written in hexameter quatrains.

But conventional meter was used, too, and most effectively, in such pieces as "The Heart of the Bruce," a ballad by the Scottish professor William E. Aytoun. This recounts the adventures of a band of one hundred knights who are taking the heart of King Robert to bury it in the Holy Land, because he had not been able while alive to strike a blow for God under the Cross. They arrive in Spain in time to help the Christians under King Alonzo defeat the infidel Moors. In so doing their leader, Lord James Douglas, throws the king's heart far ahead of him so that it will be first in the battle and then goes forward to die upon it of his injuries. Now that Robert's heart has struck its blow for God, it can be buried in Scotland. Here are the simple and eloquent concluding stanzas:

> We lifted thence the good Lord James,
>   And the priceless heart he bore;
> And heavily we steered our ship
>   Towards the Scottish shore.
>
> No welcome greeted our return,
>   Nor clang of martial tread,
> But all were dumb and hushed as death,
>   Before the mighty dead.
>
> We laid our chief in Douglas Kirk,
>   The heart in fair Melrose;
> And woful men were we that day—
>   God grant their souls repose! [48]

3. *Ballads of Bravery*

Among the most successful ballads of adventure are those which dramatize the courage of individuals in times of crisis. Browning has two short narratives of this kind which are usually reprinted in any selection from his poetry. "Incident of the French Camp" is a brief drama of a mortally wounded soldier who falls dead after faithfully delivering his message to his beloved emperor, Napoleon. "How They Brought the Good News from Ghent to Aix" is the equally famous story of three men, three horses, and a ride which saves a city. Somewhat similar is Thornbury's "The Cavalier's Escape," but in this the narrator is the pursued and the other two horsemen

are the pursuers. The cavalier pauses to strike down his ene-
mies and then arrives safely at Salisbury town.

Fortitude in the face of certain death is another quality
celebrated by the literary balladists. In "The Two Meek
Margarets," by the Scottish Victorian John Stuart Blackie, an
older woman and a younger one submit to drowning by a
Popish captain rather than swear allegiance to King James.
And in Alfred Austin's "The Death of Huss" a brave man
calmly goes to the stake accused of heresy. Thomas Chatter-
ton's long ballad "The Bristowe Tragedie" is also of this class.
In it Sir Charles Bawdin remains firmly loyal to King Henry
and is executed by King Edward.

MISCELLANEOUS BALLADS (G)

Except for the humorous ballads and parodies (type H),
which will be separately treated in chapter 5, the miscellane-
ous ballads are the final group. It is not one of the largest
categories, but it is useful and it serves as a reminder that lit-
erary balladry, like its folk and broadside relatives, can never
be absolutely confined within set limits. Since the category
exists as a catch-all, I will simply give a few samples of the
material which finds its way here.

In William R. Spencer's "Beth Gêlert," Llewelyn comes
home from hunting to find his favorite hunting dog with
bloody jaws and his baby son missing. Horrified, he destroys
the dog and then discovers the body of a wolf, which the dog
had killed, and finds his baby hidden out of harm's way. Jean
Ingelow's "Winstanley" is the story of the first builder of the
Eddystone Lighthouse, whose persistent work against mighty
odds earned him the eternal gratitude of seafaring men. And
Robert Southey's "The Battle of Blenheim" is as good an
argument against war as many a longer essay. In human terms
the famous victory meant only anguish and death and a skull
to be picked up by a questioning child nearly a century later.

The modern poets have been particularly adept at writing ballads difficult to classify, and this, of course, is in keeping with the tendency towards experimentation in all contemporary literature. Where else but here would one place Hardy's "A Dance at the Phoenix"? It tells of a former girl of the regiment who steals away from home and husband one night, at the age of fifty-nine, and dance for hours with the soldiers, as she had done years before. She returns home happy and dies that night from the strain. And in Hardy's "A Practical Woman" another wife makes a decision. Having had a series of defective sons, she goes away for several years and returns with a healthy boy, having "found a father at last who'd suit." Another unusual piece is Kipling's "Cain and Abel: Western Version," which turns the story of the first murder into an argument between a cattleman who needs water for his herds and a farmer who has dammed the water for his crops. The tale is told in what Kipling regarded as Western American dialect.

As I trust the foregoing analysis has demonstrated, the arrangement of pieces according to subject matter is enormously helpful in the study of balladry. Where works of known authorship are concerned, as in literary balladry, classification by subject matter is less vital than in the study of folk and broadside balladry. But it does serve to establish relationships which might otherwise escape the reader. The knowledge of a literary ballad's close relatives and ancestors is often helpful in producing the full appreciation of a poet's intention and his artistry.

3

The Archaic Literary Ballad

A GOOD many ill-considered statements have been
made about the impossibility of successfully imitating
the style of the British folk ballad. For any such statement to
be meaningful, we must know exactly what kind of folk text
is meant and what is regarded as a successful imitation. As has
been demonstrated, the term *folk balladry* comprises many
different types and subtypes of verse narrative. It should also
be obvious that no literary work can exist as an entity unless it
differs in some respects from all other works. The literary bal-
lad, then, must at the same time be both different from and
related to its prototypes. Any critical evaluation of the result
must be based on a recognition of these like and unlike quali-
ties.

By far the largest number of literary ballads are archaic in
that the poets have imitated older balladry, particularly that
of the folk, consciously adopting the style or the subject mat-
ter or both, of an earlier age. These archaic ballads are, in the
main, also romantic. In fact, many of those qualities by which
we identify romantic literature (supernaturalism, emotional-
ism, emphasis on adventure, Gothicism, and so on) are per-
fectly embodied in certain of the most memorable folk ballads.

Predictably the most successful authors of archaic literary ballads are poets of strong romantic interests. It does not follow, however, that the chief poets of the Romantic period are the best balladists. Almost the reverse is true. One important determinant of success is the seriousness with which the poet studies and assimilates the balladry of the people. Also important is the willingness of the poet to yield his natural desire for originality to the requirements of the genre, and this both the greatest of the poets and many of the lesser ones have been unwilling or unable to do. The literary balladist must walk a narrow line between excessive dependence on his models and too drastic departure from them. And he must remember that his finished product will be judged not merely as an imitation but as a poem which is his alone.

The most successful archaic literary ballads, like their folk prototypes, have proved themselves able to survive major changes in poetic taste, while their inferior counterparts have been forgotten. Most of the reasons for success or failure can be stated with some confidence. Unlike the early imitators and experimentalists in ballad techniques, we now have sufficient perspective to recognize some of those traits which give folk balladry its enduring appeal. The following characteristics may be regarded as of major importance:

1) Impersonality of expression (the author remains far in the background);

2) Simple, unaffected folk language (poetic diction is not usually at home in the ballads);

3) Familiar and evocative imagery (the ballad cliché is highly connotative);

4) Succinctness (the ballad story leaves much unsaid);

5) Direct and violent actions and reactions (ballad characters are uninhibited);

6) Dramatization rather than summary of events (ballads are miniature plays which use much dialogue).

But as has been shown in chapter 1, these qualities which

give the traditional ballads distinction are not usually found in the broadsides. In fact, a typical broadside is more likely to show their opposites. Yet their subject matter is similar to that of the folk ballads and they appeal to similar audiences. This leads me to conclude, with the aid of supplementary evidence, that the aesthetically pleasing qualities which I have listed have, in the main, been imposed upon the ballad in tradition. That is, I think they are largely the unconscious contributions of the folk. This theory has nothing to do with the old idea of communal authorship, which is fortunately extinct among ballad scholars. There must have been an individual author for every folk ballad. But it would be a most unusual author who could revise his work as tradition would revise it. Specifically I mean that tradition produces impersonality by removing evidence of individual authorship. Where the author has used colorful or original language, the folk will substitute familiar words and expressions. Where the author has told his story in full detail, the folk will tend to eliminate description, exposition, and even minor elements of narration to produce a story that is considerably briefer than the original and often harder to follow. Sudden and violent action will tend to be emphasized; thought and reflection will disappear. Dialogue, being dramatic, will remain and increase in prominence. All this will not, of course, make a fine ballad out of a poor one, but it will produce a text that sounds traditional. Evidence that this sort of thing does take place is conveniently provided by those broadsides which have lived in both worlds. We have various examples of original broadsides texts which display typical broadside qualities and other examples of the same ballads after they have had a life in tradition. Such texts often show the qualities which we connect with folk balladry.

Where the literary balladists have not distinguised clearly between folk and broadside texts, they have shown an inclination toward the fuller broadside manner. This is especially true of the eighteenth-century poets, who tended to regard the

folk texts as cruder than the broadsides, as indeed they some-
times were, at least where technical regularity and currency
of diction were concerned. The poets had not yet learned to
recognize the beauties of the folk manner, either because so
many of the ballads were in the subliterary Scottish dialect
or were quite obsolete, having been derived from old manu-
scripts. It was only when an eighteenth- or early nineteenth-
century author tried to complete a folk text, as Percy and
Scott did on various occasions, or when he tried to pass off
something of his own as traditional, that he attempted to re-
produce what he regarded as crude folk style. And even then
he was likely to give himself away by frequent departures
from folk idiom.

But it would be wrong to give the impression that folk
balladry necessarily combines the virtues listed for it with
uniformly effective poetic expression. An examination of some
of the less familiar texts in the Child collection will show
that the average ballad could not be given high rank if re-
garded solely as a poem. With a few notable and widely re-
printed exceptions, folk balladry as a whole contains relatively
little good poetry. And this is natural and inevitable when
we remember that it has been in the possession of the folk,
who are, of course, not poets. Folk ballad texts are almost in-
variably collected in an unpolished state. For example, the text
may contain irregular lines, missing passages, garbled phrases,
and illogical statements. Few editors of popular collections
have been able to resist revising, combining, rewriting, and
otherwise tampering with received texts. Both Percy and Scott
followed this procedure, usually without precise acknowledg-
ment of their alterations. Editors continue to do this sort of
thing and may even sound rather truculent about it, as Robert
Graves does when he defends the practice:

Usually . . . I have combined several versions, choosing the
most telling stanzas, or phrases, from each; and where all versions
are obviously defective at some point or other, owing to the mutila-

tion of a manuscript, or the poor memory of singers, I have re-
stored the missing lines in the spirit of the original. . . .

Ballads are nobody's property, and if careless singers or illiterate
printers have claimed the right to spoil them, who can deny us
the right to guess how the originals went? Not even the scholars—
though they seldom risk a guess themselves.[1]

This is not the place to discuss Graves's assumptions about
ballad originals. The important point is that he represents a
view that is now two centuries old, namely that folk balladry
must be "improved" before it is suitable for the general reader.
Thus the British poets, except when they were in direct con-
tact with folk tradition, have almost invariably imitated texts
already partially brought into line with poetic orthodoxy. This
is worth remembering when the customary remarks are made
about the impossibility of imitating "genuine folk style." As
any dependable scholarly collection will show, the uniformly
poetic and the genuine rarely merge. No poet striving for the
best possible expression within his medium would deliberately
create unpoetic, crude, awkward, and banal passages. These
are the unavoidable concomitants of tradition, and they may
contribute to the charming artlessness of a folk text. But they
could hardly be looked upon in the same light if they were
intentionally contrived by a literary balladist for the printed
page. The scholarly student of balladry, the person listening
to a folk singer, and the poet all have different expectations,
different critical responses, and different criteria of excellence.
Then there is the matter of originality. The folk prefer the
old to the new; the cliché, whether or not it is poetically effec-
tive, to the unfamiliar expression; ordinary diction to a strik-
ing coinage. But the poet has the responsibility of lifting his
poem above the usual level of folk expression without sacri-
ficing ballad virtues.

Finally we should remember that the folk ballad tends to be
archaic because of its long traditional life; it preserves old
locutions, old beliefs, old mores. Thus a poet is not likely to

feel at home with it unless it is a part of his heritage. So it is that a convincing imitation of a traditional text is both difficult and poetically unnatural. And since such a text would normally be full of flaws in artistry, most poets would probably think the effort not worth making.

Thus for many reasons the archaic literary ballad does not necessarily coincide with what we may regard as purest and best in folk balladry. The form it may take with any one poet will depend on his interests, his concepts of balladry, his literary preferences, his background, and, of course, his poetic talents. But whatever the final product may be, it will always represent a compromise between the art of the people and that of the poet.

The reader should be open-minded enough to accept as literary ballads a variety of poems based on ballad models. There is no reason, for example, to insist that the poet confine himself to the manner of the Scottish romantic ballad. On the other hand, we must be just as demanding of excellence in this genre as in any other. As it happens we are frequently disappointed. Joseph Ritson, on the title page of his *Pieces of Ancient Popular Poetry*, has an apt quotation from Skelton: "To make suche trifels it asketh some counnyng." [2] And Henry B. Wheatley has this to say in his edition of Percy's *Reliques:*

A good ballad is not an easy thing to write, and many poets who have tried their hand at composition in this branch of their art have signally failed, as may be seen by referring to some of the modern pieces in this book, which Percy hoped would atone for the rudeness of the more obsolete poems. [3]

I might add that although Wheatley's remarks were made a century ago and applied specifically to eighteenth-century literary ballads, they are no less valid today. I can think of no comparable poetic genre which has been tried by so many authors with so little complete success.

It took the literary balladists a long time to learn that form and style are at least as important as story in recapturing the flavor of old balladry. What makes such eighteenth-century pieces as Mallet's "William and Margaret," Goldsmith's "The Hermit," and Percy's "The Friar of Orders Gray" so unsatisfactory to the modern reader is the substitution of ephemeral eighteenth-century poetic conventions for those well established by tradition in the prototypes. What Mallet has done, for example, is to use the supernatural event of the return of the girl's ghost to build up the pathos of her fate. This leads inevitably to concentration upon the ghost's state of mind and almost destroys the narrative and dramatic elements. Moreover, the author fills his poem with the clichés of second-rate eightenth-century poetry ("sable shroud," "silver dew," "faithless swain"), so that he loses all the advantages of crisp, evocative ballad idiom. The poem was widely praised, however, apparently because readers and other poets admired its warmth, sentimentality, and smoothness of expression in an age when so much poetry was harshly satiric. Observe how rhetorical and unballadlike it is:

> "Bethink thee, William, of thy fault,
>   Thy pledge and broken oath:
> And give me back my maiden vow,
>   And give me back my troth.
> . . . .
> "How could you say my face was fair,
>   And yet that face forsake?
> How could you win my virgin heart,
>   Yet leave that heart to break?" [4]

"William and Margaret" seems to have been quite influential in sending early ballad imitation off on the false trail of sentimentality and moralizing. An early example of this influence is given by a piece called "G——e and D——y" (London, 1743), "in imitation of William and Margaret." [5] Here the villainy of the ghost's former lover is explained in a note: "By being hurried about in a coach, and as often over-walked, she miscarried, when five months gone with child, and died the next day." Once the ghost is introduced, the ballad consists entirely of her denunciatory monologue, which continues for twenty-six stanzas. The "young Lady of Quality" who is credited on the title page with the authorship of this piece did well to remain anonymous.

Goldsmith's "The Hermit" was first published in *The Vicar of Wakefield*, although it had been privately printed and circulated a few years before. Here the girl disguised as a pilgrim is seeking news of her lover from a hospitable hermit, who speaks in part as follows:

> "Then turn to-night, and freely share
> Whate'er my cell bestows;
> My rushy couch and frugal fare,
> My blessing and repose.
>
> "No flocks that range the valley free,
> To slaughter I condemn;
> Taught by the power that pities me,
> I learn to pity them:
>
> "But from the mountain's grassy side
> A guiltless feast I bring;
> A script with herbs and fruits supplied,
> And water from the spring.
>
> "Then, pilgrim, turn; thy cares forego;
> All earth-born cares are wrong:
> 'Man wants but little here below,
> Nor wants that little long'." [6]

The remoteness of this piece from the language of balladry is obvious. And when the speaker suddenly embraces the girl and vows undying love, this action pretty much nullifies his character as a hermit, which the author has built up with some

care. The result is unsatisfactory either as didactic poetry or
as balladry.

Percy's "The Friar of Orders Gray" is even more sentimen-
tal. The friar, who is actually the girl's lover, reports his own
death and gets a satisfactorily emotional reaction:

> And art thou dead, thou gentle youth!
> And art thou dead and gone!
> And didst thou die for love of me!
> Break, cruel heart of stone!

But the "friar" comforts her:

> O weep not, lady, weep not soe;
> Some ghostly comfort seek;
> Let not vain sorrow rive thy heart,
> Ne teares bedew thy cheek.[7]

The dialogue continues in this vein for many stanzas. The
pace of the ballad is much too leisurely; it is all talk and no
action. The diction is generally flat and trite, although Percy
has used some phrases appropriate to balladry, such as "green
grass turf," "kirk-yard wall," "my true-love dyed for me," and
"redder than the rose." But he uses too many of the old phrases
of conventional love poetry.

None of these pieces could stand today on their own merits
as literary ballads. They are interesting primarily as indica-
tions of eighteenth-century ballad taste—for they were much
admired—and they show clearly that ballad style was not re-
garded as worthy of imitation.

The sentimental ballad was followed toward the end of the
eighteenth century by a rash of horror balladry immediately
inspired by translations from the German which had them-
selves been based partly on the English models in Percy's
Reliques. Like the fad of the Gothic romance of the same
period, that of the horror ballad is not grounded in any at-
tempt at the artistic presentation of meaningful human experi-
ences but exists solely to shock the reader with gruesome fic-

tion and legends. Sir Walter Scott, who was responsible for helping to spread the fad, sums up the matter succinctly in commenting on *Tales of Wonder:*

> The supernatural, though appealing to certain powerful emotions very widely and deeply sown amongst the human race, is, nevertheless, a spring which is peculiarly apt to lose its elasticity by being too much pressed on, and a collection of ghost-stories is no more likely to be terrible, than a collection of jests to be merry or entertaining.[8]

Southey's "The Old Woman of Berkeley" may be taken as one of the more effective examples of this type of literary ballad. The story is of a woman whose debt to the devil is so great that nothing can protect her from him after death. Southey found the story told in Latin in the "monkish chronicle" of Matthew of Westminster. It was said to have happened in the year 852. A few stanzas should suffice for illustrative purposes:

8 "I have 'nointed myself with infants' fat;
   The fiends have been my slaves;
   From sleeping babes I have suck'd the breath;
   And, breaking by charms the sleep of death,
   I have call'd the dead from their graves.

9 "And the Devil will fetch me now in fire,
   My witchcrafts to atone;
   And I, who have troubled the dead man's grave,
   Shall never have rest in my own."

She asks her children, the monk and the nun, to chain her coffin to the church floor, to have fifty priests say mass for her for three days, and to perform other protective acts. On the third night the defenses are destroyed:

39 And the tapers' light was extinguish'd quite;
    And the Choristers faintly sung;
    And the Priests, dismay'd, panted and pray'd,

And on all Saints in heaven for aid
They call'd with trembling tongue.

40 And in He came with eyes of flame,
    The Devil, to fetch the dead;
    And all the church with his presence glow'd
    Like a fiery furnace red.

42 And he bade the Old Woman of Berkeley rise,
    And come with her master away;
    A cold sweat started on that cold corpse,
    At the voice she was forc'd to obey.

45 The Devil he flung her on the horse,
    And he leap'd up before,
    And away like the lightning's speed they went,
    And she was seen no more.

46 They saw her no more; but her cries
    For four miles round they could hear;
    And children at rest at their mothers' breast
    Started, and scream'd with fear.[9]

This poem, as is usual with literary balladry, is far too long. The thirty stanzas describing the Devil's assaults on the church become tiresome before the climax is reached. And there is a kind of flamboyance here that goes beyond the reader's tolerance. Southey did not have the good taste to tone down the material from his source but kept such extravagant details as having fifty priests to say Mass. The poem entirely lacks either restraint or suggestive power. And yet it does contain suspense, vivid descriptive passages, and violent action. The last few stanzas even have some emotional impact. On the whole, the poet's language is adequate if not memorable. In dealing with witchcraft and certain means of combating it, Southey chose a subject of some folkloristic interest. Yet the story is so remote from either experience or belief as to be practically meaningless to the average adult reader of the author's day or of our own.

But the faults observable in Southey's ballad, which are mild compared with those in many of the horror pieces, should not be taken to warrant a blanket indictment of the supernatural in balladry. Man's religious nature, his deeply rooted awareness of the mysteries of life, his desire for greater power and knowledge, and his occasional dissatisfaction with an earthbound and limited existence—these and other motivating forces can explain the appeal of the supernatural in the literary ballads as in other literary works. The supernatural occurrences of popular balladry were, of course, grounded in folk belief and made their appeal to the people on that basis. Obviously, this type of appeal could not be made to the sophisticated readers of ballad poetry. When the supernatural is used in literary balladry for purely thematic purposes, as in the voices from the grave in Hardy and Housman, there is no problem. And readers are also likely to be sympathetic to the author who treats the supernatural respectfully and in the traditional manner. But if a poet shows himself to feel superior to his material or actually scornful of the very beliefs on which his ballad is founded, he can hardly expect an intelligent reader to take it seriously.

Southey is the perfect example of the poet whose ambivalent attitude weakens his art. He did not know whether to laugh at the legends he used or to treat them seriously, and he was complimented rather than insulted when told that his supernatural balladry showed that he was basically a comic artist. He even tried to defend "The Old Woman of Berkeley" as a success because it frightened children in Russia, not realizing how damning it was that it did not frighten their parents.[10] Coleridge, on the other hand, was on much firmer ground. In hoping for a willing suspension of disbelief, he recognized the duality of man's response to the unknown and tried to get at truth by means of myth and parable. This essentially religious or philosophical approach has been widely used in literature (as in Elizabethan tragedy, the Christian epic, and the narrative poetry of the Romantics) and is entirely at home in literary balladry. The poet and the reader agree to accept the supernatural as a means toward truth. This is the main reason why some supernatural literary ballads speak to the mind and heart.

So much has been said and written about "The Rime of the Ancient Mariner" since its first publication in the *Lyrical Ballads* of 1798 that one hesitates to add anything to this confusing mass of material. Obviously this is not the place to discuss either the mind of Coleridge or the symbolism of the poem. My observations will be confined to the poet's use of ballad techniques.[11]

While the poem may be called a literary ballad if we stretch the term to include pieces of considerable length and complexity, it is clearly not a direct imitation of any folk or broadside ballad type. Furthermore, while the outward experiences narrated in the poem are marvelous and striking, it is the inward result of these upon the mariner that the critics have come to recognize as of prime importance. This alone differentiates the poem from the typical ballad, which ignores psychological results except as they are reflected in action. But the horrible experiences through which the mariner must pass as a result of his crime as well as the more ordinary events of the story are narrated in ballad form and style.

The opening stanza establishes the ballad tone:

> It is an ancient Mariner,
> And he stoppeth one of three,
> "By thy long grey beard and glittering eye,
> Now wherefore stopp'st thou me?" [12]

The archaic diction, the abrupt beginning, and the unassigned dialogue are all familiar from folk balladry. The first description of the mariner is conveyed indirectly through dialogue. As early as the third stanza we are given our first taste of the supernatural:

He holds him with his glittering eye—

and lest the reader overlook this, the marginal gloss states, "the Wedding Guest is spellbound by the eye of the old seafaring man, and constrained to hear his tale."

Stanzas six, seven, and the first half of eight show clearly Coleridge's ability to exploit the ballad to advance his story with extreme rapidity:

> "The ship was cheered, the harbour cleared,
> Merrily did we drop
> Below the kirk, below the hill,
> Below the lighthouse top.
>
> The Sun came up upon the left,
> Out of the sea came he!
> And he shone bright, and on the right
> Went down into the sea.
>
> Higher and higher every day,
> Till over the mast at noon—"

The events and places referred to in stanza six reflect the passage of at least several hours, while those in stanza seven suggest days and weeks and prepare the reader for reaching the equator in the next two lines.

Other features of the popular ballad include the childlike simplicity of some of the language, the frequent use of dialogue, as in the colloquy between the spirits in part 4, the dramatic presentation of important events like the arrival of the skeleton ship, and the tension-charged atmosphere of the entire poem.

Coleridge displays extraordinary skill in adapting the ballad stanza to descriptive purposes. Four successive quatrains from part 2 are among the most familiar in English literature:

> All in a hot and copper sky,
> The bloody Sun, at noon,

> Right up above the mast did stand,
> No bigger than the Moon.
>
> Day after day, day after day,
> We stuck, nor breath nor motion;
> As idle as a painted ship
> Upon a painted ocean.
>
> Water, water, every where,
> And all the boards did shrink;
> Water, water, every where,
> Nor any drop to drink.
>
> The very deep did rot: O Christ!
> That ever this should be!
> Yea, slimy things did crawl with legs
> Upon the slimy sea.

Usually he avoids the ballad clichés, but in the description of Life-in-Death he makes good use of them in achieving an effect of horror:

> *Her* lips were red, *her* looks were free,
> Her locks were yellow as gold:
> Her skin was white as leprosy,
> The Night-mare Life-in-Death was she,
> Who thicks man's blood with cold.

Here the simile "white as leprosy" alters everything that has gone before it.

The average reader is probably unaware that Coleridge was writing in the tradition of the horror ballad, especially since he tended to tone down the horror elements in later revisions. In the first edition the stanza just quoted was preceded by one which makes even more use of gruesome detail. This description is of Death:

> *His* bones were black with many a crack,
> All black and bare, I ween;
> Jet-black and bare, save where with rust

> Of mouldy damps and charnel crust
> They're patch'd with purple and green.[13]

Most would agree that the deletion of this stanza was wise. In general, horror seems most effective when it is not too explicit and when the reader's imagination is brought into play. The detail of the stanza just quoted may be compared with the starkness of the following stanza, which is much purer balladry:

> The body of my brother's son
> Stood by me, knee to knee:
> The body and I pulled at one rope,
> But he said nought to me.

"The Ancient Mariner" is a poem of 143 stanzas, of which approximately one-fourth are of five or six lines. Thus it is far longer than a typical ballad of any kind and is much more complex in its number of major incidents, its division into seven parts, and its concentration upon the changing reactions of the narrator. But although the final structure is much more elaborate than that of any ballad, it is built to a considerable degree with the bricks and mortar of balladry.

Walter Scott's "The Eve of St. John" may serve as a transitional piece between the horror ballad and the Scottish folk ballad. Appropriately, it appeared both in *Tales of Wonder* and in *Minstrelsy of the Scottish Border*. The story deals with a Scottish baron who returns home after three days' absence looking as if he has been engaged in a deadly fight. He inquires of his little foot-page about his lady's actions and learns that she has met an armed knight beside the watchfires and has invited him to her bower. But the knight has replied in these terms:

> " 'I cannot come; I must not come;
> I dare not come to thee;
> On the Eve of St. John I must wander alone:
> In thy bower I may not be.' "

But she insists, saying, "I conjure thee, my love, to be there," and explains that her husband is away with the bold Buccleuch and the priest has gone to say mass for a slain knight.

> "He turn'd him around and grimly he frown'd,
> Then he laugh'd right scornfully—
> 'He who says the mass-rite for the soul of that knight,
> May as well say mass for me:
>
> " 'At the long midnight hour, when bad spirits have
>   power,
> In thy chamber will I be.'
> With that he was gone, and my lady left alone,
> And no more did I see."

At the baron's insistence the boy reveals that the knight is Sir Richard of Coldinghame, and the baron replies:

> "The grave is deep and dark—and the corpse is stiff and
>   stark—
> So I may not trust thy tale."

Much troubled, the baron goes to his lady, who also seems disturbed. That night her lover suddenly appears at her bedside and speaks in reply to her anguished warning to leave:

> "By the Baron's brand, near Tweed's fair strand,
> Most foully slain, I fell;
> And my restless sprite on the beacon's height,
> For a space is doom'd to dwell.

She asks if he is saved and gets this reply:

> "Who spilleth life, shall forfeit life;
> So bid thy lord believe:
> That lawless love is guilt above,
> This awful sign receive."

> He laid his left palm on an oaken beam;
> His right upon her hand:
> The lady shrunk, and fainting sunk,
> For it scorched like a fiery brand.[14]

The ballad ends with the rather undramatic disclosure that the lady and her husband spend the rest of their lives as nun and monk.

This is far above the usual level of the horror ballad in that Scott makes excellent use of details appropriate to the border setting and includes much folklore connected with the appearance of supernatural beings on St. John's or Midsummer Eve. The restless spirit of the murdered man who has not been avenged, his appearance in the lady's bower, his sudden vanishing, all these are familiar folk elements. Even the beacon fire at which the lady meets him is suitable because ritual fires are connected with Midsummer Eve.

No one coming across "The Eve of St. John" without the author's name appended would suppose that it was a traditional ballad. Its structure is too elaborate, its detail too circumstantial, and its artistry too polished for that. Moreover it makes more use of local color and folk belief than would be found in any one ballad of tradition. But it does several things which our earlier examples have not done. It presents characters who are essentially like those of traditional balladry, even to the little foot-page who is loyal to his master at the expense of his mistress. It tells a compressed and well-motivated story with close attention to psychological probabilities and it shows respect for and makes use of language and incident typical of British folk balladry. Here at last we find a literary ballad worthy of attention as a work of art. In the eighteenth century, only Coleridge in "The Ancient Mariner" used ballad techniques to better advantage.

A poem which seems designed throughout as an exact imitation of the Scottish folk ballad is James Hogg's "Lord Derwent: a Fragment." Hogg was, of course, closer to the ballad tradition in his origins than Scott and may well represent the kind of rural genius responsible for the original composition of various folk ballads. However this may be, "Lord Derwent" has some of the fullness of detail and even redundancy which we can observe in various broadsides. Despite the word "fragment" in the title, the poem has thirty stanzas of ballad meter. As a means of testing my theory that tradition imposes various folk ballad qualities by pruning away unessential and inappropriate passages, I have tried the purely mechanical experiment of dropping entire stanzas from this piece. The elimination of half a dozen stanzas near the beginning of the poem and a few later on clearly results in a more effective folk ballad. Here, for example, are the first six stanzas:

1 "O why look ye so pale, my lord?
      And why look ye so wan?
   And why stand mounted at your gate
      So early in the dawn?"

2 "O well may I look pale, ladye;
      For how can I look gay,
   When I have fought the live-long night,
      And fled at break of day?"

3 "And is the Border troop arrived?
      And have they won the day?
   It must have been a bloody field,
      Ere Derwent fled away.

4 "But where got ye that stately steed,
      So stable and so good?
   And where got ye that gilded sword,
      So dyed with purple blood?"

5 "I got that sword in bloody fray,
      Last night on Eden downe;
   I got the horse and harness too,
      Where mortal ne'er got one."

6 "Alight, alight, my noble lord;
      God mot you save and see;
   For never till this hour was I
      Afraid to look on thee."

The ballad actually gains in mood and effect without a corresponding loss in sense if the third, fourth, and fifth stanzas are deleted. And other passages, particularly those in which Hogg slips from folk to poetic speech are better omitted. This is but one of various indications of the extreme difficulty of imitating the folk manner.

But to get on with the story, the lord warns his lady to prepare to follow him and then disappears. At that, their foot-page arrives from the battle to report that he has been with her lord at his gallant fight to the death against the overwhelming Scottish forces. (The ballad is narrated from the English point of view.) The following stanzas show how effectively Hogg could at times recreate the ballad idiom:

16 "Why do you rave, my noble dame,
    And look so wild on me?
  Your lord lies on the bloody field,
    And him you'll never see.

21 "How dare you lie, my little page,
    Who I pay meat and fee?
  The cock has never crowed but once
    Since Derwent was with me.

28 She turned her head to Borrowdale;
    Her heart grew chill with dread;—
  For there she saw the Scottish bands,
    Kilpatrick at their head." [15]

The ballad comes to a close with a foreshadowing of death.

Our reaction to "Lord Derwent" is likely to be that it is an entirely convincing imitation of a folk ballad but that in manner and matter it takes us only where we have often been before. Something more is needed, either real poetry or a new and original story, or perhaps both, to evoke real admiration for a literary ballad.

William Motherwell's "The Fause Ladye" seems clearly superior to "Lord Derwent" in poetic intensity, economy, and dramatic impact. While it is somewhat more polished than a typical text received from tradition, it is not obviously "literary." I give the text in full partly to indicate how difficult it would be to distinguish such a piece from a traditional ballad which had received editorial attention.

"The water weets my toe," she said,
"The water weets my knee;
Haud up, Sir Knicht, my horse's head,
If you a true luve be!"

"I luved ye weel, and luved ye lang,
Yet grace I failed to win;
Nae trust put I in ladye's troth
Till water weets her chin!"

"Then water weets my waist, proud lord,
The water weets my chin;
My achin' head spins round about,
The burn maks sik a din—
Now, help thou me, thou fearsome knicht,
If grace ye hope to win!"

"I mercy hope to win, high dame,
Yet hand I've nane to gie—
The trinklin' o' a gallant's blude
Sae sair hath blindit me!"

"Oh! help!—Oh! help!—If man ye be
Have on a woman ruth—
The waters gather round my head
And gurgle in my mouth!"

"Turn round and round, fell Margaret,
Turn round and look on me—
The pity that ye schawed yestreen
I'll fairly schaw to thee!

"Thy girdle-knife was keen and bricht—
The ribbons wondrous fine—

'Tween every knot o' them ye knit
Of kisses I had nine!

"Fond Margaret! Fause Margaret!
You kissed me cheek and chin —
Yet, when I slept, that girdle-knife
You sheathed my heart's blude in!

"Fause Margaret! Lewde Margaret!
The nicht ye bide wi' me —
The body, under trust, you slew,
My spirit wends wi' thee!" [16]

In Motherwell's poem the reader will notice the effective use of incremental repetition, which is often a feature of folk balladry, in the repeated references to the rising water. The author uses ballad meter and the Scots dialect to advantage, and he has compressed his story to such an extent that one wants to ask questions about it. We wonder, for example, why the lady murdered the knight, just as we wonder why Edward murdered his father in the well-known folk ballad. Thus the poet has successfully avoided the literary balladist's usual pitfall, excessive detail. While Motherwell's story is original in this form, it is built of such well-established ballad ingredients as the faithless loved one, the secret murder, and the revenant who is mistaken for a living person. The language is an expert blending of actual ballad clichés and other locutions constructed in the ballad manner. In a sense, however, an author deserves only partial credit for the success of such a piece as this. Some of its effect undoubtedly springs from the reader's conditioned response to a type of poetry which has long had romantic appeal.

As an example of a literary ballad in the archaic folk style, "The Fause Ladye" comes much closer to justifying itself than "Lord Derwent" and is one of the best of the avowed and unpretentious imitations. Yet even this piece, with its tense drama and vivid phrasing, leaves one vaguely dissatisfied. In this connection some comments by Edward Lytton on the literary ballads of Schiller are appropriate:

> We have the more drawn the reader's notice to these distinctions between the simple ballad of the ancient minstrels, and the artistical narratives of Schiller because it seems to us, that our English critics are too much inclined to consider that modern Ballad-writing succeeds or fails in proportion as it seizes merely the spirit of the ancient. . . . But this would but lower genius to an exercise of the same imitative ingenuity which a school-boy or a college prizeman displays upon Latin Lyrics . . . in which the merit consists in the avoidance of originality. The Great Poet cannot be content with only imitating what he studies: And he succeeds really in proportion not to his fidelity but his innovations . . . that is, in proportion as he improves upon what serves him as a model.[17]

While I would be unwilling to give the successful imitator so little credit as Lytton does, I feel that his main point is vital to any discussion of literary balladry. The pieces we most admire are always, in one way or another, more than mere imitations. While we recognize the uncommon talent which an author like Motherwell displays, we cannot help wondering whether he has contributed enough from his own genius to the poem. No such doubts arise in connection with a ballad like the following, which achieves its effects not by any novelty of idiom or poetic brilliance but by telling with real artistry a story one is not likely to forget.

"The Tower of St. Maur," by Agnes M. F. Robinson, a very minor poet, is one of the most striking of literary ballads. It may serve to illustrate the type of folk ballad imitation which uses the old style with new story matter. Here the setting is the Scottish border, and the characters and incidents are appropriate to a time in the distant past. As the ballad begins, a mother is inquiring about her little boy.

> 1   "Where's my little son, Nourrice,
>   And whither is he gone?

> The youngest son of all I have,
> He should not gang alone."

The nurse replies that his father, St. Maur, has taken him to watch the masons build the tower. The scene shifts to the boy as he asks his father why the tower and the wall beside the river need to be so thick and strong. The father answers:

> 9 "God knows the tower had need be strong
> Between my foes and thee!
> Should once Lord Armour enter, child,
> An ill death would ye dee."

He recalls Lord Armour's raids of long ago:

> 12 "And once I found my nurse's room
> Was red with bloody men . . .
> I would not have thy mother die
> As died my mother then."

And he explains that the wall must be thick to keep the autumn floods from washing it and the tower away. A gipsy mason says that he knows a spell "gars any tower to stand," but he dares not say what it is. After much persuasion, the gipsy reveals the spell:

> "St. Maur, you'll build your christened child
> Alive into the wall."

The father turns away in anger and starts home with the boy, but the waters begin to rise, and the bugle of Armour is heard in the distance. The boy asks a question.

> 31 "And will they slay my mother, then,
> That looks so bonny and small?"
> "Come back, come back, thou little lad
> To the masons at the wall."

The gipsy reminds St. Maur of his seven other sons, takes the child, and pretends to play a game with him:

40   "You'll stand so still and stark, my lad,
       You'll watch the stones that rise;
       And I'll throw in your father's sword,
       When they reach above your eyes.

41   "And if you tire o' the play, my lad,
       You've but to raise a shout:
       At the least word o' your father's mouth,
       I'll stop and pluck you out."

The ballad rises in emotional intensity as the wall rises around
the boy:

45   "O father, lift me out, father!
       I cannot breathe at all,
       For the stones reach up beyond my head,
       And it's dark down i' the wall."

But the father will not speak and the work is finished:

48   "Gang home, gang home in peace, St. Maur,
       And sleep sound if you can;
       There's never a flood shall rock this tower,
       And never a mortal man.

50   "You'll say he fell in the flood, St. Maur,
       But you'll not deceive yoursel',
       For you've lost the bonniest thing you had,
       And you'll remember well." [18]

"The Tower of St. Maur" makes excellent use of numerous
ballad characteristics without depending on stock situations.
The Scottish dialect is used with the lightest possible touch,
the language throughout is suitably direct and natural, and
ballad idiom subtly permeates the poem. The setting is ex-
pertly integrated with the plot, for the ruthless feuds of the
border did result in the massacre of entire families and did
require the strongest possible defenses. There is a faint remi-
niscence of "Lamkin" (Child no. 93) here. Lamkin the mason,
who has not been paid for building Lord Wearie's castle, is

admitted to it by a false nurse and murders the lord's baby and then his wife. There is nothing subtle in the folk ballad, no pulling of conscience between two evils, but the piece is brutal and powerful in impact. "The Tower of St. Maur" is much more complex psychologically. The reader is skillfully prepared to accept St. Maur's weakness by having him recall with horror his mother's death and by emphasizing his love for his wife, his large number of sons, and his own fearfulness. The black gipsy serves various functions. He is a logical character to deal in magic and foretell the future. Like many of his race, he is a skilled artisan, the builder of the fatal wall, the one who moves the story to its climax. At first he is the devilish tempter; later he becomes the voice of conscience. He knows the rules of his black art, as he shows when he says that only the blood of an innocent child will keep the wall standing. And he knows human nature, too, in saying that he will throw the father's sword into the wall, for this symbol of his courage will be of no further use to him. Despite its length, the ballad never flags in interest, and the suspension of disbelief which it requires is automatically granted. It is a tribute to the author's skill as an imitator that we respond emotionally to this ballad as we do to the folk ballads. We may grant that the piece contains little meritorious poetry and still claim that it is a great literary ballad on the grounds that in conception and execution it could hardly be improved upon.

If "Lord Derwent" represents an old story told in the old way, and "The Tower of St. Maur" a new story in the old manner, then Swinburne's literary ballads illustrate old stories told in new ways. He seems far less interested in originality of plot than in the art of raising the ballad stanza to a high poetic level. "The Witch-Mother" does tell a story new to English balladry, that of the abandoned mistress who murders her sons and feeds them to their unsuspecting father, but the story motif is old and seems unoriginal.[19] The ballad contains only sixteen stanzas, a very few for Swinburne, who often allows his virtuosity to overcome his art. Except for the last stanza, the ballad is narrated from the woman's point of view; the first half depicting her anguish, the second her horrible revenge. The beginning of the poem shows how the poet subtly transforms the ballad stanza by substituting metaphor and symbol for action:

> "O where will ye gang to and where will ye sleep,
> Against the night begins?"
> "My bed is made wi' cauld sorrows,
> My sheets are lined wi' sins.
>
> "And a sair grief sitting at my foot,
> And a sair grief at my head;
> And dule to lay me my laigh pillows,
> And teen till I be dead.
>
> "And the rain is sair upon my face,
> And sair upon my hair;
> And the wind upon my weary mouth,
> That never may man kiss mair.
>
> "And the snow upon my heavy lips,
> That never shall drink nor eat;
> And shame to cledding, and woe to wedding,
> And pain to drink and meat.
>
> But woe be to my bairns' father,
> And ever ill fare he:
> He has tane a braw bride hame to him,
> Cast out my bairns and me."

It is only in this fifth stanza that the poet reverts to ballad directness and simplicity. The aggrieved woman goes to the "burnside," conjures up the devil, and pledges her soul to him. Presumably he advises her to murder her sons and feed them to their father, but the poet, who concentrates throughout on the feelings of the mother, proceeds directly to her looking her sons in the eyes for the last time, slaying them, and mixing their flesh with water and their blood with wine. Wherever possible Swinburne uses what sound like typical folk ballad clichés:

> She looked fu' lang in their een, sighing,
> And sair and sair grat she:
> She has slain her young son at her breast
> Her auld son at her knee.

The climax of the ballad comes when with the bitterest irony she gives her former lover his meal:

> Says, "Eat your fill of your flesh, my lord,
> And drink your fill of your wine;
> For a' thing's yours and only yours
> That has been yours and mine." [20]

When her lord realizes what she has done, he strikes her head from her body and falls dead from grief.

Swinburne usually embroiders his ballads with sensual and sensuous details, and as Professor C. K. Hyder observes in his excellent survey of these poems, he "likes a scabrous situation." [21] In such stanzas as the following from "Lord Scales," a story of illicit love derived partly from "Little Musgrave and Lady Barnard," (Child no. 81), there is more emphasis upon sexuality and emotionality than in most folk balladry. Lord Scales's wife weeps for the danger to her lover, Lord Randal, whom she has freed from prison to be with her:

> He kissed her on her twa fair breasts,
> And hard upon her chin;
> He kissed her by her white halse-bane
> The little salt tears fell in.

> The small tears fell about her face
> Between her lips and his;
> From side to side of her gold hair
> Her face was full sad to kiss.

In the Child ballad, Lord Barnard kills Little Musgrave and then his wife, but Swinburne allows the interloper to triumph.

Parallel stanzas from the two ballads show how little but how significantly Swinburne has altered the text. In the Child ballad:

> The first stroke that Little Musgrave stroke,
> He hurt Lord Barnard sore;
> The next stroke that Lord Barnard stroke,
> Little Musgrave neer struck more.[22]

In Swinburne's version:

> Lord Scales he strak a fu' straight straik,
> But Randal strake a sair;
> Lord Scales had little joy of it,
> But Lady Helen had mair.[23]

But the preceding stanza is crude compared to the following three from "The Sea-Swallows," which displays Swinburne's unique talent for taking a ballad commonplace, in this case the legacy of tragedy like that in "Edward," and transforming it into evocative poetry. This beautifully lyrical ballad strongly suggests that the girl has borne her father's son and hence has nothing to offer all three of them but death.

> "O what will ye give my son to eat,
> Red rose leaves will never make wine,"
> "Fen-water and adder's meat."
> The ways are sair fra' the Till to the Tyne.
>
> "Or what will ye get my son to wear?"
> (Red rose leaves will never make wine)
> "A weed and a web of nettle's hair."
> The ways are sair fra' the Till to the Tyne.
>
> "Or what will ye take to line his bed?"
> (Red rose leaves will never make wine)
> "Two black stones at the kirkwall's head."
> The ways are sair fra' the Till to the Tyne.[24]

With such highly evocative language as this, the literary ballad needs no apology.

The effect of Swinburne's ballad imitations, like those of the Pre-Raphaelites generally, is static and lyrical rather than dramatic and narrative. With his extraordinary sensitivity to sound, mood, and song, Swinburne was able to extract from the romantic traditional ballad those qualities which on occasion raise it from verse to poetry. He makes much more use of color imagery, parallelism, incremental repetition, and descriptive detail than is found in tradition. He seems to have recognized, as most ballad imitators have not, that emotion rather than action is the wellspring of poetry—that poetry is not spontaneously generated by slavishly imitating the ballad manner but that the poet must use the best resources of his art. One always feels that Swinburne's standards of art were high and that in his view a ballad should offer an experience in beauty as well as an example of narrative technique. He extracts from the ballad such qualities as the following and concentrates upon them: an intolerable human situation (incest, betrayal); a lyrical expression of anger, jealousy, or grief; and dramatic events of great intensity and finality (murder, suicide). But in handling these materials he tends to use indirection, metaphor, and suggestion to cast a romantic haze over the starkness of his tale. He never forgets that the traditional ballad is a song, and he lets his verse flow smoothly as a song does, whereas a printed traditional ballad often seems verbally rough and awkward. Swinburne is, in short, the great craftsman of archaic literary balladry.

For examples of a fourth type of folk ballad imitation, that in which both the story and the telling of it seem original, we may turn to the work of Swinburne's friends, William Morris and Dante Gabriel Rossetti. In summarizing the tenets of the Pre-Raphaelite School of painters, Morris said that a picture should be naturalistic (a representation of nature, as opposed to academic or conventional), should tell a story, and should be "ornamental," that is, "it ought also to have a definite, harmonious, conscious beauty." The art, he said, was called Pre-

Raphaelite because its closest relationship was with Pre-Renaissance or Gothic art, in which he found the qualities named as well as a fourth, which he called "romantic." [25] When the Pre-Raphaelite painters turned to poetry it was entirely natural that the old balladry should appeal to them because it displayed all these ideal traits.

Emphasis on scenes or pictures and a medieval background, or at least one remote in time, are the most outstanding features of the balladry of these poets. While the narrative element in some of Morris's ballads tends to be vague, as in "Two Red Roses Across the Moon," "The Sailing of the Sword" shows no such weakness. Although in form a dramatic monologue spoken by an unhappy girl, the ballad is sufficiently impersonal in substance to let the events speak for themselves. The medieval atmosphere is conveyed in part by knights, a falcon, and a castle. Each of three sisters says farewell to her knight when the ship leaves. The first girl is dressed in scarlet, the second in russet brown, and the speaker in white. Two of the knights offer to return with presents, but Lord Roland, the narrator's love, turns his back on her. The *Sword* eventually returns bringing happiness for her sisters but tragedy for herself. The ninth of the eleven stanzas and the last one will illustrate the poet's technique:

> Lord Robert brought a ruby red,
>   *When the Sword came back from sea;*
> He kissed Alicia on the head —
>   "I am come back to thee;
> 'Tis time, sweet love, that we were wed,
>   *Now the Sword is back from sea!"*
> . . . .
> My heart grew sick, no more afraid,
>   *When the Sword came back from sea;*
> Upon the deck a tall white maid
>   Sat on Lord Roland's knee;
> His chin was pressed upon her head,
>   *When the Sword came back from sea!* [26]

Alicia's scarlet gown and the red ruby Robert brings her seem symbolic of their already consummated love, just as the whiteness of the speaker's gown indicates her virginity and that of the tall white maid who replaces her. The refrains of the second and sixth lines, with suitable variations, are used most effectively, both as emotional reactions and structural units. The folk ballad device of incremental repetition is well handled both in the refrains and in those series of three in which the characters and events are presented. Finally, the whole poem is a succession of carefully realized scenes, any or all of which could be painted from the information provided.

Two of the most famous of literary ballads are Rossetti's "The Blessed Damozel" and "Sister Helen." The former, which Oswald Doughty calls "decorative and sentimental," [27] is largely static and descriptive and owes little to traditional balladry. But "Sister Helen" is another matter. While it is an original and impressive work of art, it is clearly related to folk tradition.

Rossetti seems to have adapted his stanzaic form and dialogue pattern from the best-known text of "Edward" (Child no. 13), that given Percy by Sir David Dalrymple. The first stanza reads like this:

> "Why dois your brand sae drap wi bluid,
> Edward, Edward,
> Why dois your brand sae drap wi bluid,
> And why sae sad gang yee O?"
> "O I hae killed my hauke sae guid,
> Mither, mither,
> O I hae killed my hauke sae guid,
> And I had nae mair bot hee O."

"Sister Helen," a dialogue between a young woman and her much younger brother, begins as follows:

> "Why did you melt your waxen man,
> Sister Helen?
> Today is the third since you began."

"The time was long, yet the time ran,
Little brother."
(*O Mother, Mary Mother,*
Three days today, between Hell and Heaven!) [28]

The poet has removed the purely repetitious lines and has replaced the last line with italicized matter, which varies constantly from stanza to stanza and serves as a bit of interior monologue, applying sometimes to the boy's thought, more often to Helen's. The sixth line remains constant throughout the ballad. This stanza proves remarkably flexible in conveying the thoughts of the characters and in providing pictorial and narrative details.

Helen's former lover, who has married someone else, is suffering the torments of hell through the agency of her witchcraft. One by one the members of his family ride up to plead with her to spare Keith of Ewern. The first brother, Keith of Eastholm is followed by Keith of Westholm, who brings from Ewern two tokens of fidelity familiar in balladry:

22   "He sends a ring and a broken coin,
Sister Helen,
And bids you mind the banks of Boyne."
"What else he broke will he ever join,
Little brother?"
(*O Mother, Mary Mother,*
No, never joined, between Hell and Heaven!)

His brothers are followed by their once-proud old father, who kneels and begs for the release of his son's soul. But Helen remains adamant and revels scornfully in their misery. Finally in a part of the ballad which Rossetti added many years after its first appearance, he brings the series of pleaders to a climax by having a lady arrive:

31   "Her hood falls back, and the moon shines fair,
Sister Helen,
On the Lady of Ewern's golden hair."

> "Blest hour of my power and her despair,
> Little brother!"
> (*O Mother, Mary Mother,*
> *Hour blest and bann'd, between Hell and Heaven!*)

Soon all hear a dying knell, and the three men ride off hurriedly, carrying the lady on Westholm's horse. The image of Ewern has now melted completely. Only one question remains:

> 42 "Ah! what white thing at the door has cross'd,
> Sister Helen?
> Ah! what is this that sighs in the frost?"
> "A soul that's lost as mine is lost,
> Little brother!"
> (*O Mother, Mary Mother,*
> *Lost, lost, all lost, between Hell and Heaven!*)

As Janet Camp Troxell shows in her variorum edition of this supreme Pre-Raphaelite ballad,[29] Rossetti labored over "Sister Helen" for many years, discussed it frequently in letters to his friends, revised it, added stanzas—in short, took it most seriously. Its deserved popularity is a tribute to his taste and care. While it is possible to object that the poem is too long, verbally complex, and contrived, these very qualities help give it beauty and power, and it is not easy to say what could be deleted without loss. As a Pre-Raphaelite poem, for example, it uses to excellent effect the moonlight on a windy night as it shines upon the white mane of Eastholm's horse, the white plume of Westholm's, the white hair of their father, and finally the golden hair of the bride. As a study in human nature, it expresses in a dozen ways the cruel agony in Helen's heart. The poem is far more poetic and artistic than any folk ballad; every stanza shows craftsmanship of a high order, and the relation of the parts to the whole is expertly developed. "Sister Helen" has suggestive power, beauty, emotional impact, and magic atmosphere, yet its relative subtlety and complexity would be out of place in folk balladry. The constantly changing refrain alone would be enough to confuse any singer. Thus as a work of art it may be said to exploit the possibilities of the ballad without being bound by its limitations.

Some idea of the difficulties involved in tracing out the relationships between a specific literary ballad and the pieces which helped inspire it may now be indicated. It will be recalled that Chart C divided the supernatural ballad, type A, into various subtypes and gave examples of single folk and broadside ballads and their literary ballad counterparts. Usually such a one-to-one relationship oversimplifies the matter.

CHART D

Some Possible Sources for Rossetti's "Sister Helen"

from Chart B		
Ballad Influences	"Edward"	stanzaic pattern dialogue within family murder by the title character the "curse of hell" legacy
	? "The Maid Freed from the Gallows"	the succession of riders
	Border balladry	setting and local color family or clan loyalty
	Love balladry	opposition of lover's family the broken token and coin the forsaken girl
	? James Hogg's "Mess John"	someone tortured by means of an image
Folkloristic Influences		witchcraft, including delight in evil the lost souls
Historical & Other Influences		Christian allusions and concepts
Literary Influences		sophisticated poetic techniques

SISTER HELEN

In "Sister Helen," for example, we can trace motifs common to a number of different literary and nonliterary ballads, and we can suggest other influences from literature and folklore. Chart D, on the facing page, logically develops from Charts A, B, and C to suggest the possible ancestry of a particular ballad.

In "The Maid Freed from the Gallows" (Child no. 95), which Rossetti may have known, the members of a girl's family ride up to the gallows one by one only to respond to her pleas by saying that they have come to see her hanged. Finally her true love appears with gold and sets her free. Clan loyalty is observable in such a ballad as "Jock o' the Side," where some borderers go on a dangerous mission to rescue their kinsman. The motif of the broken token or ring occurs in various traditional broadsides, such as "Pretty Fair Maid" (Laws no. N 42), and the opposition of a lover's proud family is a motivating force in dozens of ballads. While Chart D lists a good many elements found in Rossetti's poem, it is certainly not a complete statement of its ingredients, nor does it take us far in an analysis of it. But it is helpful in suggesting that the art of the literary ballad is considerably more complex than it may appear.

One advantage which a piece like "Sister Helen" or "The Sailing of the Sword" has over pieces in archaic dialect is that both author and reader feel at home in the idiom of the poem. Whatever loss there may be in antique flavor is made up for by the sense of naturalness which current idiom inspires. Even where archaic language does appear, the most successful poems are those in which no barriers are raised to the reader's understanding. By way of summary it may be said that the outstanding archaic literary ballads are those in which the authors go beyond the simplest requirements of the type to produce clearly original works which have individual integrity and undoubted literary merit. Mere imitation, no matter how skillful or convincing, is never enough.

4

The Contemporary
Literary Ballad

AMONG the important practitioners of the art of the literary ballad have been those poets who have used the popular forms along with timely or timeless subject matter and contemporary idiom. Such poets avoid the main hazard of ballad imitation, that of speaking in an antique and unfamiliar language; and they have the advantage of using a popular and inherently dramatic means of telling a story.

In choosing modern idiom and story, the poet loses almost all the glamorous trappings of the older balladry. The lords and ladies, the medieval or at least remote setting, the obsolete moral codes, the charm of cliché and dialect—these and other romantic features must be abandoned. For many readers these are the identifying marks of balladry. How then is the reader to regard the contemporary ballad as based on established forms? The answer lies, of course, in broadside balladry, which has largely determined the character of the contemporary literary ballad. This fact would have been clear enough in earlier days when the broadside was as familiar a phenomenon as the daily newspaper. But now we tend to forget how completely its influence was felt in the two preceding centuries. Even today the influence of the broadside dominates traditional balladry on both sides of the Atlantic. Many of the older folk ballads are still sung, but numerically they represent only a small fraction of the texts which have been collected in recent decades.

Once they decided to speak in current idiom and to use broadside ballad models, the poets ran into trouble. At best, the quality of the average broadside ballad was well below that of acceptable poetry, and the parodists were always making fun of the plodding, semiliterate broadside manner. And yet the usual language of poetry was inappropriate to ballad imitation. This dilemma led to a variety of attempts to take advantage of the ballad's virtues as a narrative medium without sacrifice to the poet's sense of art. In these attempts, which spread over two centuries, we can observe the evolution of various concepts of the contemporary ballad. In roughly chronological order, with the usual overlapping, they may be described as follows:

1) Imitations of broadside balladry in which the poet uses simple language and attempts, often unsuccessfully, to avoid poetic diction. Such stories are likely to be sympathetic and tender accounts of unhappy events. (Example: Wordsworth's "Lucy Gray.")

2) Imitations, sometimes rewritings, of broadside balladry in which the tone ranges from the cheerful to the tragic and in which the poets exploit the ballad's wide variety of style and subject. (Examples: Burns's "The Lass that Made the Bed to Me" and Kipling's "The Ballad of East and West.")

In types 1 and 2, the significance of the story is largely conveyed by the events recounted. That is, these ballads are generally unsophisticated and straightforward and they mean what they say. Usually they are mildly romantic in tone.

3) Imitations of both the contemporary broadsides and the folk ballads in which the story may be taken as a poignant commentary on the fate of man. Here the theme becomes more important than the incident, and the philosophy of the

author seems to determine the choice of subject matter. These ballads may be either romantic or realistic. (Example: Housman's "Bredon Hill.")

4) Imitations of the broadsides which emphasize sordid and depressing aspects of contemporary life. In these pieces the author is usually detached and impersonal, as in the folk ballads. Such poems are generally realistic. (Example: Auden's "Victor.")

In types 3 and 4 the ballads are relatively sophisticated and subtle. They usually imply considerably more than they state and are heavily ironic.

I.

Of these types, the first now seems most dated and open to serious critical objections. At the moment we are conditioned to believe that the author should not be too obtrusive in fiction but that his story should speak for itself. Thus we tend to react against the sentimental in balladry, particularly if it is presented melodramatically.

An example of a ballad of the first type is offered by "Bryan and Pereene: a West Indian Ballad," which Percy prints in the *Reliques*. He says that the story is founded on fact and that he "owes the following stanzas to the friendship of Dr. James Grainger, who was an eminent physician in that island St. Christopher's when this tragical incident happened." The less ambiguous table of contents lists Grainger as the author. Here are the key stanzas:

> 1 The north-east wind did briskly blow,
>   The ship was safely moor'd;
>   Young Bryan thought the boat's-crew slow,
>   And so leapt over-board.

> 2 Pereene, the pride of Indian dames,
>   His heart long held in thrall;

> And who so his impatience blames,
>   I wot, ne'er lov'd at all.

10 Her fair companions one and all,
        Rejoicing crowd the strand;
    For now her lover swam in call,
        And almost touch'd the land.

11 Then through the white surf did she haste,
        To clasp her lovely swain;
    When, ah! a shark bit through his waste: [sic]
        His heart's blood dy'd the main!

12 He shriek'd! his half sprang from the wave,
        Streaming with purple gore,
    And soon it found a living grave,
        And ah! was seen no more.

13 Now haste, now haste, ye maids, I pray,
        Fetch water from the spring:
    She falls, she swoons, she dies away,
        And soon her knell they ring.

14 Now each May morning round her tomb
        Ye fair, fresh flowerets strew,
    So may your lovers scape his doom,
        Her hapless fate scape you.[1]

It is not hard to see why the editors included this piece in *The Stuffed Owl: an Anthology of Bad Verse*.[2] In its way, the story is simply told, but the language is that of the parlor pastoral rather than the tragic broadside. And somehow the climax, which should be terrible, verges on the ludicrous, probably because the author was incapable of suiting his diction to his subject matter. Some of his weakness is clearly displayed in his use of "ah!" in stanzas 11 and 12. It would be hard to imagine a more inadequate sound in those circumstances.

Wordsworth's ballads were much lower keyed and usually dealt with quiet rural tragedies. Fortunately he realized his own limitations in this field, as the following stanza shows:

> The moving accident is not my trade;
> To freeze the blood I have no ready arts:
> 'Tis my delight, alone in summer shade,
> To pipe a simple song for thinking hearts.[3]

Thus he avoided the stories of violence and horror which were so popular during his early poetic career and dealt instead with life and death among lowly people of good character.

Wordsworth's "Lucy Gray" owes nothing to folk balladry but could not have been written without his knowledge of broadside style. The ballad tells of a little girl who is sent by her father with a lantern to lead her mother home from town. Lucy loses her way in a sudden snowstorm, and her mother, who has arrived home without her, joins the father in an all-night search. They find only her footprints, which disappear suddenly on a bridge. The poem contains three recognizable styles. The first, which may be called Wordsworthian, is found in stanza two:

> No mate, no comrade Lucy knew;
> She dwelt on a wide moor,
> — The sweetest thing that ever grew
> Beside a human door!

A second style displays typical eighteenth-century artificiality:

> 7 Not blither is the mountain roe:
>   With many a wanton stroke
> Her feet disperse the powdery snow,
>   That rises up like smoke.

And the third style is that of the plodding broadside ballad:

> 8 The storm came up before its time:
>   She wandered up and down;

> And many a hill did Lucy climb:
> But never reached the town.

9   The wretched parents all that night
     Went shouting far and wide;
     But there was neither sound nor sight
     To serve them for a guide.

13   And then an open field they crossed:
     The marks were still the same:
     They tracked them on, nor ever lost;
     And to the bridge they came.

If the poet never rose above this level in "Lucy Gray," one could only conclude that the ballad was a corruptive influence, but he recovers control and brings the piece to an imaginative conclusion by suggesting that somehow Lucy has walked into immortality and may still be seen upon the moors:

16   O'er rough and smooth she trips along,
     And never looks behind;
     And sings a solitary song
     That whistles in the wind.[4]

Stanzas 8, 9, and 13 illustrate two related points about broadside ballad imitations: 1) the reader who does not recognize the broadside style may simply feel that the poet has lost control of his medium, and 2) the poet who uses such a style should try to make certain that his control will not be questioned.

It will be recalled that in the 1800 preface to *Lyrical Ballads* Wordsworth quotes Dr. Johnson's famous ballad stanza:

> I put my hat upon my head,
> And walk'd into the Strand,
> And there I met another man
> Whose hat was in his hand.

He then proceeds to quote what he calls "one of the most justly admired stanzas" from "The Children in the Wood":

> These pretty Babes with hand in hand
> Went wandering up and down;
> But never more they saw the Man
> Approaching from the Town.

He goes on to say, among other things, "the one stanza we admit as admirable, and the other as a fair example of the superlatively contemptible." And he concludes that Dr. Johnson's stanza is bad because the "matter" is contemptible.[5] Professor Albert Friedman sees in stanza 8 of "Lucy Gray," "Wordsworth's own attempt to imitate the admired simplicity" of the stanza from the broadside ballad.[6] Unfortunately for Wordsworth's argument, the quatrain from "The Children in the Wood" is only a shade better than Johnson's and his own stanza is at the same low level.

In using the simple language of the contemporary broadside, Wordsworth and presumably his predecessors were consciously avoiding the artificialities of eighteenth-century poetic diction. They used, in short, the real language of men as that language was used in the broadsides. This, in essence, is what led Wordsworth to all the confusing and much-discussed statements about poetry and prose and about the suitability of the language of the common man for poetic expression. What Wordsworth ignored in these statements of theory, though fortunately he did not always ignore them in practice, was one fact that should have been obvious, namely that there was no necessary connection between poetry and the speech of the common man. More important was the fact that the broadsides were almost completely devoid of poetry. Wordsworth's admiration of the quoted stanza from the broadside ballad sprang not from any poetic merit but from his tender response to the fate of the children. Finally he ignored the fact, though he demonstrated it often enough in his poems, that poetry is very different from prose in its architectonics. The subtle craftsmanship of such a poem as "The Solitary Reaper" is a far cry from the near banality of a ballad imitation like "We Are Seven." In short, Wordsworth presents the curious paradox of one of England's truly great poets being misled by the appealing and unaffected simplicity of some broadside ballads into mistaking prosaic verse for poetry.[7]

More successful than Dr. Grainger's poem and more consistent in style than Wordsworth's is "Jemmy Dawson" by William Shenstone. This deals with a contemporary event of great importance, the final, fatal attempt of 1745 to return the house of Stuart to the throne. Percy prints the following explanation with the ballad:

James Dawson was one of the Manchester rebels, who was hanged, drawn, and quartered on Kennington Common in the County of Surrey, July 30, 1746. — This ballad is founded on a remarkable fact, which was reported to have happened at his execution. . . .

The first ten stanzas tell of Dawson's being led astray by party strife and turning against his king, and they include his true love's urgent wish that mercy rather than justice should obtain. But the harsh sentence of death is carried out while she watches:

13 She followed him, prepar'd to view
The terrible behest of law;
And the last scene of Jemmy's woes
With calm and steadfast eye she saw.

14 Distorted was that blooming face,
Which she had fondly lov'd so long:
And stifled was that tuneful breath,
Which in her praise had sweetly sung:

15 And sever'd was that beauteous neck,
Round which her arms had fondly clos'd:
And mangled was that beauteous breast,
On which her love-sick head repos'd:

16 And ravish'd was that constant heart,
She did to every heart prefer;
For tho' it could his king forget,
'Twas true and loyal still to her.

17   Amid those unrelenting flames
     She bore this constant heart to see;
     But when 'twas moulder'd into dust,
     Now, now, she cried, I'll follow thee.[8]

And in two more stanzas he brings the ballad to a close. In such terms as "blooming face," "beauteous breast," and "constant heart" we observe the poet's dependence on the staples of poetic diction, but at the same time there is nothing fanciful about what is happening. When the breath is literally stifled and the heart ravished, the trite associations do not apply, and the reader is made aware of some of the horror of the execution. Since Dawson's cause had failed and he was technically guilty of treason, the poet had to be circumspect in expressing his sympathy. He does so very cleverly by concentrating upon the events as seen through the eyes of a refined and devoted maiden. And after such an experience, her death from shock and grief seems well enough motivated. (That the story is said to be true is, artistically speaking, beside the point, but that report must have added considerably to its contemporary impact.) The meter here is quite regular iambic tetrameter; the poem throughout is carefully rhymed, and the expression displays a kind of simple elegance which more than two centuries have not tarnished. The style is that of the street ballad refined and ennobled by the poet's understanding of the tragedy which his story reenacts. Somehow Shenstone's taste led him safely through the hazards of this sensational material. And he never allowed himself to descend for the sake of verisimilitude to a low level of broadside style.

2.

In contrast to those poets who regarded the contemporary ballad as a means of paying tender and sentimental tribute to the victims of tragedy, we have the second group of imitators, those who were willing to accept the ballad on its own terms as a straightforward vehicle of entertainment. Robert Burns, for example, was satisfied to write or rewrite the simple stories of casual or lasting love which circulated so freely on the broadside sheets. "The Lass That Made the Bed to Me" belongs to that large class of ballads which includes such widely circulated songs as "Home, Dearie, Home" ("Bell-Bottom Trousers") and "The Foggy Dew." Two young people meet and spend the night together; the ensuing events range from the grief of abandonment to years of marital happiness. In Burns's ballad the narrator is offered lodging in the home of a maid who makes a bed for him. In describing the girl, the poet heightens conventional ballad language:

> Her hair was like the links o' gowd,
> Her teeth were like the ivorie,
> Her cheeks like lilies dipt in wine,
> The lass that made the bed to me.[9]

The next morning the girl feels that she has been ruined, but the narrator says that she may make his bed "for aye." Thus this version of the old story ends on a promise of prolonged happiness. Throughout the poem Burns uses the familiar speeches of the broadside of love but gives each phrase a smoothness and inevitability usually lacking in his models.

The broadside ballad tradition can easily bridge the gap in time between Burns and Hardy, as is seen in "The Dark-Eyed Gentleman," which is similar to the previous piece but falls into the special category happily designated "ballads of wayside seduction." In the first of only three stanzas we have the essence of the story:

> I pitched my day's leazings * in Crimmercrock Lane,
> To tie up my garter and jog on again,

* "Leazings": bundle of gleaned corn (Hardy's note).

> When a dear dark-eyed gentleman passed there and said,
> In a way that made all o' me colour rose-red,
>> "What do I see—
>> O pretty knee!"
> And he came and he tied up my garter for me.[10]

The girl's subsequent remorse is again more than compensated for by marriage. In the broadsides, the ending is more typically a lament. In "The Nightingale," for example, where the symbolism of tying up the garter is replaced by playing a tune on a fiddle, the seducer announces that he has a wife and six children at home. But in "The Foggy Dew" the story is much like Hardy's. In raising the folk idiom to poetry and a suggestion of song, Hardy shows the true poet's touch. Even the single quoted stanza is a brief playlet in which the vocabulary is both appropriate to the speaker and revealing of the characters involved.

A third example of the cheerful imitation broadside is Burns's "The Poor and Honest Sodger," which both in title and text sounds like a rewritten street ballad. The story is that of the lover who returns unrecognized, but here the subject matter which Goldsmith and Percy archaized is made contemporary or timeless. The slight sentimentality of this piece is that of the broadside type, as is the lyric note, which Burns, of course, improves upon.

> Sae wistfully she gaz'd on me,
> And lovelier was than ever;
> Quo' she, "A sodger ance I lo'ed,
> Forget him shall I never:
> Our humble cot, and hamely fare,
> Ye freely shall partake it,
> That gallant badge—the dear cockade,
> Ye're welcome for the sake o't."[11]

The wishful thinking which is so often reflected in broadside balladry makes its appearance here. When the girl discovers

that the soldier is really Willie, she reveals that her grand-
father has left her a farm and some gold. Thus they have
everything necessary to begin their life together.

But not all the ballads of this second group are so heavily
derivative. The literary ballad has long appealed to poets of
strong narrative inclination who liked a good story for its own
sake. Among English poets, Rudyard Kipling is the prime
example of the ballad writer, though, as has been shown, not
all his pieces are contemporary. T. S. Eliot, in a penetrating
essay, came to Kipling's defense and explained what he was
trying to do in his verse narratives. Eliot describes the ballad
as follows:

In the narrative Border Ballad, the intention is to tell a story in
what, at that stage of literature, is the natural form for a story
which is intended to arouse emotion. The poetry of it is incidental
and to some extent unconscious; the form is the short rhymed
stanza. The attention of the reader is concentrated on the story
and the characters; and the ballad must have a meaning immedi-
ately apprehensible by its auditors.[12]

Eliot goes on to say that the ballad has wide appeal for many
kinds of people including the highly educated, and that it is
to this large audience, rather than to the more specialized
audience of difficult poetry, that Kipling speaks. Kipling holds
the highest position among what Eliot calls verse writers and
is also and incidentally a poet, but his main intention was to
produce the kind of verse which we call the ballad. For a poet
of such strikingly different techniques as Eliot to make these
observations about Kipling is of great value in reminding us
that, despite the views of certain critics, the intention of the
poet need be neither mysterious nor inconsequential, at least
in the study of literary balladry.

Kipling's ballads range widely in scene, form, and tone, but
always the story comes first. In "The Grave of the Hundred
Head," one of his most gruesome tales, a young English lieu-

tenant is killed by a Burmese sniper, and his death is avenged by his Indian troops. They slaughter one hundred of the enemy and build a monument of heads over the grave of their officer:

> They made a pile of their trophies
> High as a tall man's chin,
> Head upon head distorted,
> Set in a sightless grin,
> Anger and pain and terror
> Stamped on the smoke-scorched skin.[13]

Thus peace comes to the river, for the Burmans have learned their terrible lesson. By telling the story from the point of view of the avengers, the author emphasizes his theme of devotion to the white subaltern, but his descriptive details also convey the horror of the deed. In addition to extraordinary control over his chosen medium, Kipling displays an uncanny ability to create and people a completely foreign setting and make the reader feel temporarily at home in it. He does this in "Danny Deever," which Eliot speaks of with admiration and which is too well known to dwell upon here. Here the story is narrated indirectly by means of dialogue, but the reader is electrified by its tense drama. Another army story, famous at least for an out-of-context quotation, is "The Ballad of East and West." This is a border ballad with an Indian setting in which the theme is honor among enemies, but the plot is of prime importance, for it is full of precipitous and heroic action. Here again Kipling shows his mastery over form by telling the story without even a stanzaic pause from beginning to end. Yet the meter is iambic heptameter rhyming *a a, b b,* etc., or in other words, each couplet is really a stanza in ballad meter. Moreover, the poet has used just enough of the phrasing of the old balladry to give his tale the familiar charm. The story is that of the colonel's son who risks his life to pursue the border thief into his hideout in an effort to recapture his father's mare. The thief so admires the young Englishman's daring that he not only returns the mare but sends his own son back as the youth's blood-brother and fellow soldier of the Queen. The ballad is as full of dialogue as many of the traditional pieces. Here is a sample:

> He has knocked the pistol out of his hand—small room
>   was there to strive,
> " 'Twas only by favour of mine," quoth he, "ye rode so
>   long alive:
> "There was not a rock for twenty mile, there was not a
>   clump of tree,
> "But covered a man of my own men with his rifle cocked
>   on his knee.
> "If I had raised my bridle-hand, as I have held it low,
> "The little jackals that flee so fast were feasting all in
>   a row." [14]

Both in phrasing and spirit, this is the language of balladry. And the poet has adapted it to its new setting with entire appropriateness. For versatility and excellence in the art of narrative, no other literary balladist comes close to Kipling.

These few examples could be greatly increased by further references to Kipling or to other poets such as Masefield, Noyes, and Tennyson. But the general class speaks for itself and requires little comment except perhaps the observation that it is far less easy to write such pieces effectively than one might suppose. Where the story itself is of major importance, any weaknesses in the telling are likely to be glaring.

But the scene of the straightforward ballad need not be exotic nor the events improbable. In one of the most charming examples of recent light verse, "A Subaltern's Love-song," John Betjeman sketches the activities of an English afternoon and evening in the country. After tea and tennis, a young couple return to the girl's home for the six o'clock news and a drink before dinner. In lilting dactyls which somehow con-

vey the precise accents of informal speech, the narrator re-
cords the details of his experience:

> The scent of the conifers, sound of the bath,
> The view from my bedroom of moss-dappled path,
> As I struggle with double-end evening tie,
> For we dance at the Golf Club, my victor and I.
> . . . .
> By roads "not adopted," by woodlanded ways,
> She drove to the club in the late summer haze,
> Into nine-o'clock Camberley, heavy with bells
> And mushroomy, pine-woody, evergreen smells
> . . . .
> Around us are Rovers and Austins afar,
> Above us, the intimate roof of the car,
> And here on my right is the girl of my choice,
> With the tilt of her nose and the chime of her
>   voice, . . .[15]

In form this owes something to the verse of music hall and
operetta, in substance to the romantic broadsides of love. But
most of all it is a clever and highly original adaptation of
balladry to the simple but meaningful events of every day.

3.

The third type of contemporary balladry is well illustrated
in a number of poems by Hardy and Housman. The quality
which dominates these pieces but is largely absent from folk
and broadside balladry is irony, the irony which arises from
one's observation of man's thwarted desires and tragic fate,
from the great gulf between his hopes and his realization of
them. While the conclusion of a popular ballad may contain
elements of the ironic, they are usually understated and in-
conspicuous. These literary ballads build toward the ironic
statement: the situation rather than the story is of prime im-

portance, and we react to the plight of the individual more than to the drama of the event. And since emphasis upon the feelings of the individual is a feature of lyric verse, we are more likely to find a lyric note in these poems than in those which emphasize deeds rather than states of mind. The term contemporary is somewhat flexible as applied to these ballads, but they are all written in modern idiom, frequently in the manner of those eighteenth- and nineteenth-century broadsides which are included in this study among the contemporary rather than archaic types.

"Farewell to Barn and Stack and Tree," Housman's no. 8 in *A Shropshire Lad*, is as close as any poet comes to combining modern diction with the evocative style and stanza of the folk ballad. The story is like that of "The Twa Brothers" (Child no. 49), which tells of one's brother's fatally stabbing the other either accidentally while wrestling or in a burst of anger. In the Scottish texts printed by Child, the story is told in the third person. In American versions of "Edward" (Child no. 13), in which the victim is brother rather than father, the story is presented as a dialogue. In Housman we have a brief dramatic monologue. Yet its half dozen stanzas are as memorable as any in literary balladry. Here is the full text:

1   "Farewell to barn and stack and tree,
       Farewell to Severn shore.
    Terence, look your last at me,
       For I come home no more.

2   "The sun burns on the half-mown hill,
       By now the blood is dried;
    And Maurice among the hay lies still
       And my knife is in his side.

3   "My mother thinks us long away;
       'Tis time the fields were mown.
    She had two sons at rising day,
       To-night she'll be alone.

4   "And here's a bloody hand to shake,
        And oh, man, here's good-bye;
    We'll sweat no more on scythe and rake,
        My bloody hands and I.

5   "I wish you strength to bring you pride,
        And a love to keep you clean,
    And I wish you luck, come Lammastide,
        At racing on the green.

6   "Long for me the rick will wait,
        And long will wait the fold,
    And long will stand the empty plate,
        And dinner will be cold." [16]

Partly because this is a monologue, the action is not dra-
matized but consists of a series of tableaux: the dead brother,
the anxious mother, the empty place at the table. This is a
departure from ballad technique, but the situation is so
fraught with drama that nothing is lost. Oddly enough, the
poem does not stand up well to logical analysis. Stanzas 1
and 4 are rather declamatory and artificial; we can't quite im-
agine that the young man would speak this way in the given
circumstances. If the blood has had time to dry (stanza 2),
the murderer has also had time to wash his hands and would
presumably have done so before talking to his friend. Fur-
thermore, stanza 4 gives a questionable image of performing
farm chores with bloody hands. Stanza 5 seems enigmatic or
unnecessary or both. Are we to assume that what the speaker
wishes for Terence he has failed to obtain for himself? And
has this lack contributed in some way to the tragedy? Then,
too, it seems unnatural for the speaker to show no signs of
remorse after killing his brother, although it is customary for
Housman's young men always to blame their stars and not
themselves. Yet despite these objections, the emotions triumph
over the mind, and the poem remains a fine literary ballad.
Like many of his poems, it passes Housman's own test for

poetry by making the skin tingle with excitement. The last stanza echoes those stanzas of "Sir Patrick Spens" which depict the bereaved ladies futilely awaiting the return of "thair ain deir lords" who have been lost at sea. Such a last stanza as Housman's is in itself a justification for the literary ballad as a type. And the last line, which is simple idiomatic English when taken out of context, bears the full weight and poignancy of the family tragedy.

"The True Lover" is an example of a typical ballad motif altered to coincide with Housman's philosophy and technique. Both the Child ballads and the broadsides contain numerous stories about young men who go calling on their true loves at night in secret, the resulting events ranging from low comedy to murder.[17] In this poem the youth has cut his throat in despair because the girl will not love him and has come to spend his last few minutes in her arms. Whether or not his actions are physically possible, this is a situation made for balladry. The second and third of the nine stanzas could hardly be improved upon. The lover has whistled softly from the dark and speaks:

> "I shall not vex you with my face
>   Henceforth, my love, for aye;
> So take me in your arms a space
>   Before the east is grey.
>
> "When I from hence away am past
>   I shall not find a bride,
> And you shall be the first and last
>   I ever lay beside."

Hardly knowing why, she goes outdoors to him and wonders why he seems not to breathe. He speaks of having "stopped the clock" for her. But suddenly we find the piece skirting close to the ludicrous. The ballad stands or falls on the seventh and eighth stanzas:

> "Oh lad, what is it, lad that drips
>   Wet from your neck on mine?
> What is it falling on my lips,
>   My lad, that tastes of brine?"
>
> "Oh like enough 'tis blood, my dear,
>   For when the knife has slit
> The throat across from ear to ear
>   'Twill bleed because of it." [18]

The dying lover's almost jocular understatement certainly contrasts too sharply with the sincere and desperate plea of the early stanzas.

Housman also makes good use of the pastoral tradition in English balladry. Ballad heroes are always meeting pretty girls in woods or fields and making love to them. In "Bredon Hill" the setting was idyllic as the young lovers lay on the hilltop and listened to the church bells on Sunday morning. But any reader of Housman might suspect that their happiness was illusory. The lover tells of his answering the summons of the bells by saying that they would go to church on their wedding day. But that winter at Christmas time his love went to church alone:

> They tolled the one bell only,
>   Groom there was none to see,
> The mourners followed after,
>   And so to church went she,
>   And would not wait for me.
>
> The bells they sound on Bredon,
>   And still the steeples hum.
> "Come all to church, good people,"—
>   Oh, noisy bells, be dumb;
>   I hear you, I will come.[19]

In the last line we again have ironic understatement, but here it is well prepared for by the metaphor in which going to church means dying, and it is doubly ironic that what once was "a happy noise to hear" now calls him to death.

The kind of irony which is indicated by such subtle juxtaposition of phrases would be out of place in folk balladry, where it would soon be blurred or disappear in tradition. The typical reader of broadsides would not be prepared for this kind of ambiguity either, and for that matter, the unsophisticated reader of poetry might be misled. (I have known students to interpret "Bredon Hill" as a story of punishment for nonattendance at church.)

Housman's ballad stories are usually timeless and could as easily be applied to antiquity as to the present day. Thus their misery and bitterness are appropriately expressed in ballad language that is both old and new, that suggests the romantic folk ballad in modern dress. The young Englishmen through whom Housman speaks are sensitive idealists who cannot help being hurt. They would have understood Shelley or Keats better than Pope or Johnson. Housman's tone of desperation and rebellion is much more prominent than the tone of stoical acceptance which appears from time to time.

With Thomas Hardy the situation is reversed. Hardy's ballads are not much more cheerful than Housman's and he is no less sympathetic toward his characters, but he manages to remain somewhat detached from the sad spectacle of human misery. For example, if any of his characters commit suicide, they are not cheered by the author as Housman's victims are. Hardy's irony is less likely to be verbal than Housman's but is no less central to the effect of his ballads. The character of his irony is in fact indicated by the title of one of his collections, *Satires of Circumstances*. In Hardy, as in Housman, things are always turning out differently from the way one would hope or expect. But where Housman's stories are timeless, Hardy's tend to be fixed in time. In fact he often indicates an approximate date from the recent past as appropriate to the action. And where Housman's characters are all much

alike and are only partially defined, Hardy's are sharply de-
lineated and extremely varied.

In selecting the forms for his ballads, it was entirely suitable
for Hardy to lean toward those of the journalistic broadsides,
which had long recorded the accidents and tragedies of ordi-
nary people. And it was also right that these dramas be re-
corded in the language of the street ballads, even if that meant
imitating at times the halting, unpoetic verse of the ballad
sheet. In this connection, John Crowe Ransom shows a mis-
understanding of Hardy's intention when he writes as follows:

First, there are the tales which are more or less on the order of
the folk-ballads. Almost always in these the tragic story is racy
and bold in its conception, and told in good order, but lacks that
vividness, and finality of phrase, that we want most desperately.
And we feel like saying that Hardy knew the behaviors of the
folk, and knew their diction too, so far as his comic purposes were
concerned . . . but did not know how they could make the
diction tragic nor how they could make it poetic. That would be
the well-kept secret of the old oral or anonymous ballads. Few of
the lettered poets have known that secret. Wordsworth did not
possess it.[20]

Ransom's remarks are typical of those whose concepts of
balladry are too limited. The fact that neither Hardy nor
Wordsworth was imitating the folk ballads destroys the valid-
ity of his comments. Furthermore, he does not seem to see the
inconsistency of wishing that Hardy had mixed the diction of
the highly romantic folk ballad of tragedy with subject matter
which Ransom elsewhere recognizes as naturalistic. And fi-
nally I might observe that much of the "well-kept secret" has
had fairly wide circulation for a century and a half.

To be specific about Hardy's technique, I shall begin with
"The Mock Wife," which tells of a dying man whose wife has
been imprisoned for poisoning him. Knowing only that he is
dangerously ill and unaware of his wife's arrest, he pleads to
give her a final kiss. His kindly neighbors find another woman

willing to perform this act of charity, and the man dies happy. Later his young wife is "strangled and burnt," though some still doubt her guilt. Hardy tells this story of two centuries before in nine quatrains of halting iambic heptameter. A couple of sample stanzas will show what he was about:

> And dying was Channing the grocer. All the clocks had
> struck eleven,
> And the watchers saw that ere the dawn his soul would
> be in Heaven;
> When he said on a sudden: "I should *like* to kiss her
> before I go,—
> For one last time!" They looked at each other and
> murmured, "Even so."
> . . . .
> And as he begged there piteously for what could not be
> done,
> And the murder-charge had flown about the town to
> every one,
> The friends around him in their trouble thought of a
> hasty plan,
> And straightway set about it. Let denounce them all who
> can.[21]

Now Hardy did not gain his reputation as one of the chief modern poets by writing this kind of doggerel. In fact he gives himself away by unintentionally rising above this general level in certain words and phrases. But he is clearly attempting throughout the poem to tell the story in the manner of a sincere but incompetent broadside versifier. To such poets, rhyme and line length were of paramount importance. Hence the pointless "All the clocks had struck eleven" in the first line quoted is used in anticipation of the trite but important reference to heaven in the second. So also in the eighth line, the final sentence is awkward and gratuitous, but it does fill an otherwise blank space. Throughout the ballad one finds such brave attempts to retain control. But what is the advantage to the poet in imitating this weakest of broadside styles? The answer must be that factual murder stories had been told in this way for three hundred years, and Hardy could think of no other style likely to give his ironic tale such an impression of verisimilitude.

As can be seen in the appendix to this study, Hardy is among the most prolific of literary balladists. We have already seen his lighter touch in "The Dark-Eyed Gentleman." More typical of his grim fatalism is "The Brother." In half a dozen trimeter quatrains, this monologue tells of a young man who thinks he is avenging his sister when he hurls her seducer to his death from Bollard Head. Later, having discovered that the two had been secretly married, he is about to commit suicide himself. This is still in the idiom of the folk, but the level of expression is considerably higher than in "The Mock Wife":

> And now I go in haste
> To the Head, before she's aware,
> To join him in death for the wrong
> I've done them both out there! [22]

In "The Forbidden Banns: a Ballad of the Eighteen Thirties," the story deals with parental opposition to a marriage and the eventual death of all involved. This type of subject is familiar from the old balladry of both main kinds and hence is appropriate for a piece in the traditional manner. Here Hardy again shows a mastery of technique. The ballad seems singable, as "The Mock Wife" or "The Brother" does not, and sounds like a broadside which has been in tradition and has acquired some of the old folk locutions. In the four stanzas of part 1, Hardy uses the broadside manner. Here the father appears in church to forbid the banns and try to prevent his son's marriage. But the deed is too much for his heart:

> Then, white in face, lips pale and cold,
> He turned him to sit down,

> When he fell forward; and behold,
>   They found his life had flown.

In part 2, the marriage has taken place. Hardy shifts to the folk style:

> 'Twas night-time, towards the middle part,
>   When low her husband said,
> "I would from the bottom of my heart
>   That father was not dead!"
>
> She turned from one to the other side,
>   And a sad woman was she
> As he went on: "He'd not have died
>   Had it not been for me!"
>
> She brought him soon an idiot child,
>   And then she brought another:
> His face waned wan, his manner wild
>   With hatred of their mother.

The folk touch is especially noticeable in the fourth and sixth lines above and in the third of these stanzas. The man now realizes the truth of his father's warnings against the marriage, and Hardy returns to the flat broadside style in bringing his melodramatic tale to a quick close:

> What noise is that? One noise, and two
>   Resound from a near gun.
> Two corpses found: and neighbors knew
>   By whom the deed was done.[23]

The stanzas in folk style refute Ransom's argument that Hardy could not make his ballad diction tragic and poetic, while those in broadside style indicate his wish to keep the whole story within a realistic framework.

If any doubt remains concerning Hardy's conscious imitation of street balladry, it should be removed by such a piece as "The Catching Ballet of the Wedding Clothes." Beneath the title appear the words "Temp. Guliel. IV." The word *ballet,* a dialectal term in both Britain and America, usually signifies the text of a ballad as it appears on a single printed sheet. The term *Catching* implies that the ballad is singable, while Hardy's placing it in the time of William IV shows that he recognized that period as the heyday of the romantic-sentimental stall ballad. The story is that of a girl who loves Jack the sailor but is wooed by a gentleman who sends her a box full of wedding clothes and a ring. The white witch to whom she has gone for advice suggests marrying Jack but using the other man's gifts. She does so and is haunted by her rich wooer, who claims her as his own. Finally she yields to the argument that

> She who wears a man's bride-clothes
> Must be the man's wife.[24]

Years later she returns, a rich lady, to muse momentarily beside Jack's grave.

The language throughout displays the semiliteracy of the man in the street who was the best customer for broadside ballads of this kind. The love triangle involving a poor sailor and a rich but unwelcome suitor is the basis of various broadside stories, but Hardy handles his narrative differently. The girl who has tried to have everything her own way is troubled, like the disloyal lovers of the older balladry, by the appearance of the one betrayed. But Hardy adds a note of complexity in suggesting that loyalty which can be so easily compromised can hardly be counted on to endure. Hence the ironic ending, which would never do in broadside balladry.

4.

Hardy and Housman take the ballad seriously as a vehicle for their ironic stories. That is, they do not satirize, distort, or otherwise exploit their narrative medium. More recent poets, on the other hand, have achieved intensified ironic effects by exaggerating certain stylistic traits of the broadsides. I am not speaking here of humorously intended ballad parodies but rather of sardonic commentaries on the fate of men and women.

No one has succeeded better at this kind of balladry than W. H. Auden. But to understand his intention, one must have some knowledge of the balladry from which his poems descend. In earlier editions of his works, the ballad now titled "Miss Gee" was known as "Let Me Tell You a Little Story." Beneath the title Auden printed, in the manner of some broadsides, "Tune: St. James' Infirmary." Now "St. James' Infirmary" is a variant of "The Bad Girl's Lament" (Laws no. Q 26) or "The Young Girl Cut Down in Her Prime," a broadside which tells the fate of one who has descended from the ale house and the dance hall to the life of a prostitute and eventually to disease and death. By an ironic contrast, Auden's heroine is a frustrated spinster whose excessive prudery leads her to conceal her cancer until too late. Her final fate is to become a cadaver for medical students. The fact that Auden refers to a tune suggests that he wanted the poem judged not in the conventional way but as an imitation of a ballad designed to be sung.

While the following excerpt does not do full justice to "Miss Gee," it indicates Auden's methods:

1 Let me tell you a little story
   About Miss Edith Gee;
   She lived in Clevedon Terrace
   At Number 83.

2 She'd a slight squint in her left eye,
   Her lips they were thin and small,
   She had narrow sloping shoulders
   And she had no bust at all.

5   The Church of St. Aloysius
    Was not so very far;
    She did a lot of knitting,
    Knitting for that Church Bazaar.

11 She passed by the loving couples,
    She turned her head away;
    She passed by the loving couples
    And they didn't ask her to stay.

15 She bicycled down to the doctor,
    And rang the surgery bell;
    "O, doctor, I've a pain inside me,
    And I don't feel very well."

21 They took Miss Gee to the hospital,
    She lay there a total wreck,
    Lay in the ward for women
    With the bedclothes right up to her neck.

23 Mr. Rose he turned to his students,
    Said, "Gentlemen, if you please,
    We seldom see a sarcoma
    As far advanced as this."

25 They hung her up from the ceiling,
    Yes, they hung up Miss Gee;
    And a couple of Oxford Groupers
    Carefully dissected her knee.[25]

Throughout the ballad the style rarely rises above a rather banal broadside level. The author remains entirely effaced and inspires sympathy for Miss Gee through his choice of personal details. Her poverty, her puritanism, her subconscious sexual frustration, and the general sterility of her life are portrayed with great skill. Yet the tone is casually ironic and even slightly humorous. Actually both this and the following poem echo the meter and phrasing of the American ballad "Frankie and Johnny," which Auden formerly indicated as the tune for the next piece and which is rather ludicrously unpoetic in places. Everyone knows that Johnnie "was her man, but he done her wrong." In Auden's poem, it is the woman who is the unfaithful one and dies as a result.

"Victor" is a carefully developed psychological study. Victor has been brought up with strong religious principles and no worldly knowledge. At the boarding house he falls in love with a loose woman who looks "as pure as a schoolgirl / On her First Communion day." When he later hears the other boarders laughing about Anna's promiscuity, he loses his grip on reality, confuses God with his dead father, who had said, "Don't dishonour the family name," and hears voices ordering him to kill his wife. He does so and is taken away believing in his own divinity. Much of the story is told in a serio-comic way, as in the following stanzas:

> They were married early in August,
> She said; "Kiss me, you funny boy":
> Victor took her in his arms and said;
> "O my Helen of Troy."

> It was the middle of September,
> Victor came to the office one day;
> He was wearing a flower in his buttonhole,
> He was late but he was gay.

> The clerks were talking of Anna,
> The door was just ajar:
> One said; "Poor old Victor, but where ignorance
> Is bliss, et cetera."

> Victor stood still as a statue,
> The door was just ajar:
> One said; "God, what fun I had with her
> In that Baby Austin car."

His bride's amused attitude toward him, Victor's romantic view of her, the gossip of the clerks, the pointless repetition of the second line in two stanzas, the rhyming of *ajar* with *et cetera*, all these show clearly that Auden is doing everything possible to exploit the techniques of vulgar balladry. Yet somehow this detracts not at all from the emotional impact of the ensuing tragedy. Auden leads the reader to respond with horror and understanding to the murder which Victor believes he must commit. Notice, too, how much may be read into the thirty-seventh and last stanza:

> Victor sat in a corner
> Making a woman of clay:
> Saying; "I am Alpha and Omega, I shall come
> To judge the earth one day." [26]

I can think of no more effective way for the poet to have told this sordid story of social inadequacy than in the ballad manner. In both these pieces as in others of the same class by different poets, one notices that authorial detachment which uses events rather than commentary upon them to guide the responses of the reader.

Louis MacNeice's "The Streets of Laredo" is another ballad based on an American folksong of British ancestry. Most people who listen to ballads at all have heard the sad story of the cowboy who has been fatally wounded in a gambling game and who asks that his mourners "beat the drum slowly and play the fife lowly" as they carry him to his grave. (Actually this ballad, "The Cowboy's Lament" [Laws no. B 1] is closely related to "St. James' Infirmary." Both descend from the English broadside "The Unfortunate Rake," the story of a young man who dies of syphilis.) In the same meter and with some similar phrases, MacNeice takes his readers on an imaginary tour of London after a bombing and fire raid in World War II. This remarkable poem is so tightly constructed that any condensation of it is damaging, but a couple of stanzas will at least give the flavor of the piece:

> O early one morning I walked out like Agag,
> Early one morning to walk through the fire

Dodging the pythons that leaked on the pavements
With tinkle of glasses and tangle of wire;

When grimed to the eyebrows I met an old fireman
Who looked at me wryly and thus did he say:
"The streets of Laredo are closed to all traffic,
We won't never master this joker today."

The fireman goes on to say that though the bank has been blown up, loot is free for the taking. Then a succession of characters appears: first a cockney who has lost everything but one rocking chair; then Sir Christopher Wren, who comes "from a wound in the asphalt" and promises to rebuild the city once more; then Bunyan and Blake, who seem to feel that God has justly punished Laredo; and finally a Wandering Jew, who has found only destruction in place of the asylum he sought. The ballad ends with a two stanza chorus in which the fire speaks:

Now ring the bells gaily and play the hose daily,
Put splints on your legs, put a gag on your breath;
O you streets of Laredo, you streets of Laredo,
Lay down the red carpet—My dowry is death.[27]

In the substance of the ballad, the poet has strayed far from his source, and in quality he rises well above it. But once more we have a ballad-inspired piece which does what no ordinary poem could do in making its sharp observations on human nature, in combining humor and pathos in its examples of folk speech, in introducing the supernatural without apology, and in creating a final effect of tragic intensity. While this poem is a most unusual and impressive achievement, it also serves to illustrate the flexibility of the ballad in accommodating itself to a variety of moods and styles.

The contemporary ballad is roughly equivalent in verse to the short story in prose. It must be without question a narrative, and often a dramatic one. It must tell a story from which the reader can derive pleasure and enlightenment. It must focus upon some significant aspect of human existence. And it must be constructed with great care to produce the desired results. Furthermore, it can tell stories with the greatest possible variety of plot, setting, theme, and character.

5

Humorous Literary Ballads and Parodies

NO one can read far in literary balladry without being struck by the number and quality of the humorous pieces. Some writers, like Thomas Hood, W. M. Thackeray, W. S. Gilbert, and Lewis Carroll, devoted themselves almost exclusively to comic rather than serious balladry. Numerous others produced both kinds. A small portion of the poems considered in this chapter are designed merely to tell amusing stories in the ballad manner, but most of them are parodies of specific ballad types or of individual pieces, folk, broadside, and literary. If the art of parody is not dead in these humorless days, it is certainly sickly, but in earlier generations and particularly in the age of Victoria it was widely and skillfully practiced.

A basic technique of parody, that of using as much as possible of an original while turning serious into ludicrous matter, is particularly adaptable to balladry because of the distinctive features of the genre. That the poets missed no opportunities to make fun of ballad locutions will be obvious from the following examples.

PARODIES OF THE ARCHAIC FOLK BALLAD

The successful parody of a particular ballad type naturally depends on the reader's recognition of stylistic peculiarities, and here the Scottish folk ballad had much to offer. In nineteenth-century Britain almost everyone knew some Scottish balladry and could appreciate the author's reshaping of it for humorous purposes. Lewis Carroll has several skillful poems of this kind. "The Lang Coortin'" makes fun of ballads describing years of devotion to absent lovers. After being away thirty years the man is greeted less than cordially, and the following dialogue ensues:

> "O didna ye get the rings, Ladye,
>   The rings o' the gowd sae fine?
> I wot that I have sent to thee
>   Four score, four score and nine."
>
> "They cam' to me," said the fair ladye.
>   "Wow, they were flimsie things!"
> Said—"That chain o' gowd, my doggie to howd,
>   It is made o' thae self-same rings."

The ballad continues at length and in a lively fashion until the lover is firmly refused and goes to seek another love. He has learned his lesson:

> "For gin I find a ladye gay,
>   Exactly to my taste,
> I'll pop the question, aye or nay,
>   In twenty years at maist." [1]

The success of this piece stems partly from its satirical distortion of romantic ballad matter but mainly from its clever adaptation of ballad language to farcical purposes. "The Wandering Burgess," though more dated, is even better. It tells of Gladstone's return to Oxford after ten years of representing another district in Parliament, and his shock at seeing the defacement of the "Tom" quadrangle by certain architectural innovations. This piece is brilliantly constructed from a succession of such archaic ballad clichés as these:

> He turned him round and round about,
>   And looked upon the Three;
> And dismal grew his countenance
>   And drumlie grew his e'e.

> "What cheer, what cheer, my gallant knight?"
>   The gate-porter gan say.
> "Saw ever ye sae fair a sight
>   As ye have seen this day?"

> "Now haud your tongue of your prating, man;
>   Of your prating now let me be.
> For, as I'm a true knight, a fouler sight
>   I'll never live to see." [2]

Unfortunately this ballad has suffered the fate of most journalistic satire. It deserves a better one.

This is true also of W. E. Aytoun's wonderful satiric ballad "The Queen in France," which, however, was well known for more than half a century from the frequent reprinting of the *Bon Gaultier Ballads,* a collection of humorous pieces by Aytoun and Theodore Martin first published in 1845. The poem, which consists of two parts with a total of sixty-five stanzas, dates from the days when Victoria was a happy young queen, wife, and mother, and when Albert still seemed a foreigner. The visit to France took place in 1843, and the ballad appeared in November of that year in *Tait's Edinburgh Magazine.* A fairly long quotation is necessary to do it justice:

> It fell upon the August month,
>   When landsmen bide at hame,
> That our gude Queen went out to sail
>   Upon the saunt-sea faem.

And she has ta'en the silk and gowd,
The like was never seen;
And she has ta'en the Prince Albert,
And the bauld Lord Aberdeen.

"Ye'se bide at hame, Lord Wellington:
Ye daurna gang wi' me:
For ye hae been ance in the land o' France,
And that's eneuch for ye.

"Ye'se bide at hame, Sir Robert Peel,
To gather the red and the white monie;
And see that my men dinna eat me up
At Windsor wi' their gluttonie."

They hadna sailed a league, a league,—
A league, but barely twa,
When the lift grew dark, and the waves grew wan,
And the wind began to blaw.

"O weel weel may the waters rise,
In welcome o' their Queen;
What gars ye look sae white, Albert?
What makes your e'e sae green?"

"My heart is sick, my heid is sair:
Gie me a glass o' the gude brandie:
To set my foot on the braid green sward,
I'd gie the half o' my yearly fee.

"It's sweet to hunt the sprightly hare
On the bonny slopes o' Windsor lea,
But O, it's ill to bear the thud
And pitching o' the saut saut sea!"

And aye they sailed, and aye they sailed,
Till England sank behind,
And over to the coast of France
They drave before the wind.

Then up and spak the King o' France,
Was birling at the wine;

"O wha may be the gay ladye,
That owns that ship sae fine?

"And wha may be that bonny lad,
That looks sae pale and wan?
I'll wad my lands o' Picardie,
That he's nae Englishman."

Then up and spak an auld French lord,
Was sitting beneath his knee,
"It is the Queen o' braid England
That's come across the sea."

"And O an it be England's Queen,
She's welcome here the day;
I'd rather hae her for a friend
Than for a deadly fae." [3]

This seems to me a remarkable achievement, requiring the utmost skill, sense of humor, tact, knowledge of balladry, and *expertise*. Every cliché falls naturally into place, and most of them are entirely appropriate. Among the many virtues of this satire as a work of art one notices the contrast, by implication, between the great deeds of the kings and queens of the old balladry with the safe and pleasant social visit of modern times. Then there is the brief Channel crossing which becomes an adventure on the "saut sea faem" for the seasick prince who gets a yearly fee, who looks like "nae Englishman," and whose idea of pleasure is rabbit-hunting. One observes also the queen's tact in leaving Wellington at home only a generation after Waterloo. The rest of the ballad deals with the imagined trivia of the visit including the Queen's indigestion from the rich French food, her boastings to the French admiral about the British Navy, and her being entertained by the minstrel singing a song composed by "Bon Gaultier." After three days she is homesick for her babies and says farewell. Despite the fact that parodies are usually ranked below serious pieces, I would place this among the best of the literary ballads.

Another satiric ballad of Aytoun's is "Little John and the Red Friar." Robin Hood is dead and his men are scattered, some having gone with Jem of Netherbee and a few remaining with Little John, who tries to retain control of Sherwood Forest. He is much incensed to hear of a red friar, who calls himself Bishop of London, and who has entered Sherwood with permission from the pope to hunt outlaws. Little John seeks and finds the monstrous friar, fights with him, and is on the point of defeat when he asks permission to blow his bugle-horn. His followers appear, but the friar has a horn, too, which produces a much larger force under Jem of Netherbee. Little John has no choice but to acknowledge the friar's power and rank and his right to remain in Sherwood. The imaginary minstrel ends his ballad nostalgically:

> So ends this geste of Little John —
> God save our noble Queen!
> But, Lordlings, say — Is Sherwood now
> What Sherwood once hath been? [4]

In its phrasing and incidents, the whole poem obviously makes fun of the Robin Hood ballads, but there is more to it than this. It is also a clever satire on a contemporary religious controversy between Lord John Russell and Cardinal Wiseman involving the creation of Catholic bishops in England.[5] That the modern reader's appreciation of the poem is not entirely dependent on historical information is a tribute to Aytoun's skill.

A parody of several folk ballads is Lewis Carroll's "The Two Brothers," which begins much like "The Cruel Brother" (Child no. 11), contains elements from Child's A version of "Edward" (Child no. 13), and for good measure has the motif of drowning from "The Twa Sisters" (Child no. 12). In Carroll's poem, when two brothers go fishing one puts a hook through the other and uses him for bait. This occasions a lively punning dialogue between the boy on the bridge and his former tormentor in the water. It is not until near the end of this piece of thirty-six stanzas that the author shifts from the jocular anapests of the music hall to the idiom of the folk ballad. But when he does, the parallels are obvious. The sister appears and speaks:

> "Oh what bait's that upon your hook,
> My brother, tell to me?"
> "It is but the fantailed pigeon,
> He would no sing for me."
> . . . .
> "Oh what bait's that upon your hook,
> Dear brother, tell to me?"
> "It is my younger brother," he cried,
> "Oh woe and dole is me.
> . . . .
> Farewell, farewell, sweet sister,
> I'm going over the sea."
> . . . .
> She turned herself right round about,
> And her heart brake into three,
> Said, "One of the two will be wet through and through,
> And t'other'll be late for his tea!" [6]

As a final example of this type, we turn again to Kipling, whose versatility with all kinds of balladry is a constant source of wonder. "The Fall of Jock Gillespie" is not the border ballad one might suppose from the title but the story of a modern clubman whose strange actions prompt his friends to question him. The ensuing dialogue is reminiscent of that between the drunken husband and the unfaithful wife in "Our Goodman" (Child no. 274):

> 2 An' syne he laughed, an' syne he sang,
> An' syne we thocht him fou,
> An' syne he trumped his partner's trick,
> An' garred his partner rue.

6   "There's a thrid o' hair on your dress-coat breast,
        Aboon the heart a wee?"
    "Oh! that is fra' the lang-haired Skye
        That slobbers ower me."

7   "Oh! lang-haired Skyes are lovin' beasts,
        An' terrier-dogs are fair,
    "But never yet was terrier born,
        Wi' ell-lang gowden hair!"

The men have guessed his secret, and it is not long before the
inevitable event occurs:

12 An' it fell when *siris*-shaws were sere,
        An' the nichts were lang and mirk,
    In braw new breeks, wi' a gowden ring,
        Oor Jockie gaed to the Kirk! [7]

PARODIES OF THE SUPERNATURAL LITERARY BALLAD

Among the more significant ballad parodies of the turn of
the nineteenth century are those connected with Lewis's
Tales of Wonder. Some of these actually appeared in that
work beside the ballads being parodied; others are included
in the clever and anonymous collection entitled *Tales of
Terror*, which is partly a parody of Lewis's volume and partly
its competitor.

Some seventy-five years after the first appearance of David
Mallet's "William and Margaret," that poem was still well
enough known to justify a parody of it. So in *Tales of Terror*
we find "The Scullion Sprite; or, the Garret Goblin. A St.
Giles's Tale. Written by a Boot-Catcher at the 'Pig and
Pepper-Box.'" The parody is a stanza-by-stanza rewriting of
Mallet's poem, with as much vulgarizing of detail as possible.
It will be recalled that the ghost of Margaret appears to de-
nounce the unfaithfulness of her former lover. Here are the
first, the fourteenth, and the last of the seventeen stanzas of
each:

William and Margaret	The Scullion Sprite
It was at the silent solemn hour,	'Twas at the hour when sober cits
When night and morning meet;	Their eyes in slumber close;
In glided Margaret's grimly ghost,	In bounced Bett Scullion's greasy ghost,
And stood at William's feet.	And pinched Tom Ostler's toes!
"But hark! the cock has warn'd me hence!	"The kitchen clock has warned me hence,
A long and last adieu!	I've other fish to fry;
Come see, false man, how low she lies,	Low in her grave, thou sneaking cur,
Who dy'd for love of you."	Behold Bett Bouncer lie!"
And thrice he call'd on Margaret's name,	And thrice he sobbed Bett Bouncer's name,
And thrice he wept full sore:	And blew his nose quite sore;
Then laid his cheek to her cold grave,	Then laid his cheek on the cold hob,
And word spake never more.	And horse rubbed never more! [8]

The quoted passages pretty much speak for themselves. Considering what he had to base his parody on, I don't see how the author could have done any better.

The horror tradition carried to its supposedly humorous extreme is represented in *Tales of Terror* by "Grim, King of the Ghosts; or, the Dance of Death. A Churchyard Tale." This is a close parody of "Monk" Lewis's "The Cloud-King" which is itself almost a parody of the horror ballad. In "The Cloud-King the castle warder tells a pilgrim the story of Romilda, who once lived there. She was so vain that she scorned even the love of kings, and she spurned the suit of "a lovely young page," declaring that she would not wed until some prince of the air courted her and promised to obey her first two commands. Unexpectedly the Cloud-King appears, accepts her terms, and elopes with the struggling girl. He is described in part as follows:

> His sandals were meteors; his blue eyes reveal'd
> The firmament's lustre, and light scatter'd round;
> While his robe, a bright tissue of rain-drops congeal'd,
> Reflected the lightnings his temples that bound.

He takes her to their wedding-feast, where his supernatural relatives, the Water-Sprite and the Erl-King, offer her refreshment:

"Hail, Queen of the Clouds! lo! we bring thee for drink
The blood of a damsel, both lovely and rich,
Whom I tempted, and left 'midst the billows to sink,
Where she died by the hands of my mother, the witch."

. . . .

"With the heart of a warrior, Cloud Queen, for thy food,
The head of a child on thy table we place: . . ."

But the Giant of Flame terrifies her even more:

"To-morrow I feast in my turn, for at morn
Shall I feed on thy flesh, shall I drink of thy blood!"

When the Cloud-King will not save her, she recalls her original bargain and knows that she will be free only if she can devise an impossible task for him. First she asks to be shown the truest of lovers, "And lo! by her side stood the lovely young page." Then comes her second command: " 'Than the *truest*, now show me a *truer!*' said she." He cannot do so, and the spell is broken. After this fairy tale, Lewis adds a playful note:

I think it necessary to explain, that my object in writing this story, was to shew young ladies that it might possibly, now and then, be of use to understand a little grammar; and it must be clear to every one, that my heroine would infallibly have been devoured by the demons, if she had not luckily understood the difference between the comparative and superlative degree.[9]

One might reasonably complain that, despite its happy ending, Lewis's poem is too gruesome. Apparently the parodist thought so. But like a cartoonist who makes a homely man hideous, the anonymous author of "Grim, King of the Ghosts" goes far beyond his original. Here again the status of the main characters is lowered for comic purposes. An old sexton tells the story, making his own daughter the heroine and Bob Brisket, the butcher's boy, the devoted lover. When he first appears to woo Nancy, Grim is described as follows:

"No flesh had the spectre, his skeleton skull
Was loosely wrapped round with a brown shrivelled skin;
His bones, 'stead of marrow, of maggots were full,
And the worms they crawled out, and the worms they
    crawled in."

The next stanza is a close parody of Lewis's description of the
Cloud-King:

"His shoes they were coffins, his dim eye revealed
The gleam of a grave-lamp with vapours oppressed;
And a dark crimson necklace of blood drops congealed,
Reflected each bone that jagged out of his breast."

Here the parodist has turned a striking picture into a hideous
one. Grim kisses Nancy, and she happily elopes with him.
They arrive at the charnel-house palace, where he invites his
friends to the wedding feast, scrawling the invitations in
blood on dead men's skin. The ghosts dance at the party and
then feast on "corpses decayed." Even this is not enough and
the author plows ahead:

"Through the nostrils of skulls their blood-liquor they
    pour,
The black draught in the heads of young infants they
    quaff;
The vice-president rose, with his jaws dripping gore,
And addressed the pale damsel with horrible laugh." [10]

The story proceeds much like the original: Nancy escapes by
verbal trickery and returns to safety and Bob Brisket.

The ballad is clever in its way but pretty revolting; it cer-
tainly fails to demonstrate that an excess of horror becomes
laughable. But it does show that a parody without true light-
ness of touch in subject matter and treatment is more likely to
expose the author's bad taste than to provide the reader with
much pleasure.

"The Rime of the Auncient Waggonere," which first ap-
peared in *Blackwood's Magazine* in February 1819, turns

Coleridge's story into a tale of roadside farce narrated by a drunken and belligerent character. The author, William Maginn, divided his story into four parts, each corresponding very roughly to a part of the original. He even included appropriate marginal glosses which comment humorously on the story as it unfolds. The waggonere is telling the tailor of a fateful trip during which his wagon fell through the ice with the loss of all the passengers' food and drink. Here is one of the better stanzas:

> "The waine is fulle, the horses pulle,
>   Merrilye did we trotte
> Alonge the bridge, alonge the road,
>   A jolly crewe I wotte;" —
> And here the tailore smotte his breaste,
>   He smelte the cabbage potte!

Because they have lost their food and drink in the icy river, the waggonere is glad to see "a goode grey goose":

> And with the butte end of my whippe,
>   I hailed it in Goddhis name.

After the goose is cooked and eaten, the passengers blame the waggonere for killing it and threaten him with jail. What seems at first like an eclipse of the sun proves to be a bumbailiff riding in pursuit. The passengers flee, and the narrator fells the bailiff. As part third opens, the tailor speaks:

> "I feare thee, auncient waggonere,
>   I feare thy hornye fiste,
> For itte is stained with gooses gore,
>   And bailliffe's blood, I wist."

The police arrive and a battle ensues, but the outnumbered waggonere is knocked out and then taken into custody. He escapes from jail and takes to the road:

> Once more upon the broad highwaye,
>   I walked with feare and drede;
> And every fifteen steppes I tooke,

> I turned about my heade,
> For feare the corporal of the guarde
> Might close behinde me trede!

The tailor is so unnerved by the story that he rushes too fast into a room, fractures his skull, and expires. Thus we arrive at the "Morale":

> Such is the fate of foolish men,
> The danger all may see,
> Of those, who list to waggoneres,
> And keep bad companye.[11]

Henry Duff Traill is little known today, but he was a prince of Victorian parodists. In "After Dilettante Concetti," which begins like "Sister Helen" and ends like one of Rossetti's sonnets from *The House of Life*, he makes delightful fun of the writing of ballad refrains of the Pre-Raphaelite type:

> "Why do you wear your hair like a man,
> Sister Helen?
> This week is the third since you began."
> "I'm writing a ballad; be still if you can,
> Little brother.
> (O Mother Carey, mother!
> What chickens are these between sea and heaven?)" [12]

At last a big brother comes in, say that "refrains have become a ridiculous 'fad,' " and denounces them in a well-turned sonnet as "a too transparent artifice to pass."

PARODIES OF BROADSIDE BALLADRY

"Thomas Ingoldsby," the Reverend Richard Harris Barham, speaks of "The Children in the Wood" as "a venerable ditty, which we have all listened to with respect and affection." We need not doubt his sincerity, though we may question the taste which led him to retell the serious broadside ballad in a farcical manner. One feels that more than mere verbal dexterity is needed to make this a funny story. At any rate, here is a sam-

ple of the way he tries to do so in "The Babes in the Wood."
The children have just been abandoned in the woods by the
kinder ruffian:

> From that moment the Babes ne'er caught sight
>   Of the wretch who thus wrought their undoing,
> But passed all that day and that night
>   In wandering about and "boo-hoo"-ing.
> The night proved cold, dreary, and dark,
>   So that, worn out with sighings and sobbings,
> Next morn they were found stiff and stark,
>   And stone-dead, by two little Cock-Robins.[13]

In the *Ingoldsby Legends* the text is accompanied by a suitably
comic cartoon of the children crying in the woods. And
Barham was not alone in rewriting this ballad. An anonymous
street balladist produced a version in a country dialect full of
lower-class slang. His equivalent passage reads as follows:

> They liv'd till next night ven they guv up the ghost,
> They vos both on 'em freezed as stiff as a post;
> A cock robin was perched on a tree close by, —
> He vept as he vitnessed those babbies die;
> Then he kivered 'em over, as nice as could be,
> Vith some cabbage leaves fresh, vot he picked off a tree.[14]

Barham's version is longer and cleverer than the street ballad
and shows some flashes of literary talent, but the modern
reader will probably not be much amused by either parody.

Of course our social sensitivity today is far greater than
that of the nineteenth century, and therefore we are likely to
be made uneasy by certain types of humor. In this connection,
one recurring feature of the older ballad parodies prevents
their full appreciation today. That is the idea that what is
tragic or at least serious in the upper classes becomes either
comic or a matter of indifference in the lower. Or to put the
matter a little differently, this attitude implies that serious

literature becomes comical almost automatically if the author lowers the rank, speech, and behavior of his characters. Thus a tailor who eats cabbage is amusing, while a wedding guest who attends a feast is not. This attitude permeates the literature of the eighteenth and nineteenth centuries, except where it is overshadowed by sentimentality. English fiction is full of it as is English drama, and to a lesser extent it appears in poetry. Wordsworth's concept of the dignity of the common man was by no means generally agreed upon. Some readers may recall Francis Jeffrey's comments on the poetry in which lower-class characters appear and are treated with respect. Of such poems by Wordsworth and his followers Jeffrey had this to say:

The love, or grief, or indignation of an enlightened and refined character, is not only expressed in a different language, but is in itself a different emotion from the love, or grief, or anger of a clown, a tradesman, or a market-wench.[15]

So it is that the "Scullion-Sprite" becomes only an object of ridicule. So too the soldiers and sailors of Thomas Hood's comic ballads are maimed and killed by the author with obvious relish, because he can use such devastating puns in narrating their difficulties. "Faithless Nelly Gray" begins this way:

> Ben Battle was a soldier bold,
> And used to war's alarms;
> But a cannon-ball took off his legs,
> So he laid down his arms.
>
> Now as they bore him off the field,
> Said he, "Let others shoot;
> For here I leave my second leg,
> And the Forty-second Foot."

Nelly rejects him because of his wounds, and Ben hangs himself:

> And there he hung till he was dead
> As any nail in town;
> For, though distress had cut him up,
> It could not cut him down.[16]

This sort of thing is undeniably clever; whether or not it is amusing is a matter of taste.

More kindly is "The Diverting History of John Gilpin," by William Cowper, a long and farcical ballad of the broadside type. It shows some condescension towards the characters, but at least it recognizes their common humanity, as many of the harsher pieces do not. No comic ballad has had wider circulation than the story of the frugal tradesman's wild ride. A few stanzas will illustrate how neatly the author controls the reader's response to the events recounted:

> John Gilpin's spouse said to her dear—
> Though wedded we have been
> These twice ten tedious years, yet we
> No holiday have seen.
>
> To-morrow is our wedding-day,
> And we will then repair
> Unto the Bell at Edmonton
> All in a chaise and pair.
>
> . . . .
> The morning came, the chaise was brought,
> But yet was not allow'd
> To drive up to the door lest all
> Should say that she was proud.

Since there is no room for John in the chaise, he must travel on a borrowed horse. But he has no sooner mounted the animal than he must dismount, for three customers have entered his shop:

> So down he came; for loss of time,
> Although it griev'd him sore,

> Yet loss of pence, full well he knew,
> Would trouble him much more.[17]

But he gets off at last, loses control of the horse, and begins his wild ride. The populace assumes that he is riding a race, turnpike men open gates for him, and he passes his family at the inn and goes ten miles beyond. Then comes the return trip, which is equally comical and unsuccessful. The ballad is lively throughout, truly humorous, and a justly celebrated example of light verse. And yet the modern reader may find the subject matter and social setting too remote from his own experience for full appreciation. When the poem first appeared in 1782, it became an immediate hit and remained popular for generations. It inspired at least one sequel, "The Railway Gilpin," which appeared in *Punch* many decades later. This tells of the original Gilpin's grandson whose family leaves him at the station because he has lost his ticket and who has a wild ride on the following express. But this is all rather forced, and it lacks both the skill and the humor of its prototype.[18]

The second canto of Byron's *Don Juan* extracts some questionable humor from cannibalism among the victims of a shipwreck, and this subject has appealed also to two distinguished comic balladists. In Thackeray's "Little Billee," the young sailor is about to be eaten by his two greedy companions when he spies land:

> "Jerusalem and Madagascar,
> And North and South Amerikee." [19]

He is saved by the British fleet under Admiral Napier. In motif this is somewhat akin to the traditional broadside "The Silk Merchant's Daughter" (Laws no. N 10), in which a girl in disguise among shipwrecked sailors including her lover is selected by lot to serve as food for the others. But a ship is sighted in time to save them all. Not so in W. S. Gilbert's "The Yarn of the 'Nancy Bell.' " Like the Ancient Mariner, an old sailor tells his tale to a stranger. He begins like this:

> "Oh, I am a cook and the captain bold,
>   And the mate of the *Nancy* brig,
> And a bo'sun tight, and a midshipmite,
>   And the crew of the captain's gig."

When his listener expresses bewilderment, he cheerfully explains that after a shipwreck and near starvation, lots were drawn and the others were eaten, one by one, until only he and the cook were left. The cook had the pot boiling for him only to be dumped into it himself:

> "And I eat the cook in a week or less,
>   And—as I eating be
> The last of his chops, why, I almost drops,
>   For a wessel in sight I see!" [20]

So it is that he can claim to be all the people named. Gilbert says in his preface that this piece, the first of his Bab Ballads, was originally submitted to *Punch* but was "declined by the then Editor, on the ground that it was 'too cannibalistic for his readers' tastes.'" As it turned out, this was not a good prophecy, but the point seems well taken.

The comic illiteracies of the two preceding pieces are mild compared with some of Thackeray's dialect poems. The following stanza, from one of the *Ballads of Policeman X*, shows more clearly how he would manhandle the language for humorous purposes:

> An igstrawnary tail I vill tell you this veek—
> I stood in the Court of A'Beckett the Beak,
> Vere Mrs. Jane Roney, a vidow, I see,
> Who charged Mary Brown with a robbin of she. [21]

Thackeray has a number of other such pieces, including several written in what he believed to be a comic Irish dialect.

While the humor of some older comic balladry is dated, it is remarkable how much of it retains its freshness and appeal. Compared with the preceding centuries, the twentieth is a barren one for the lighthearted humourous ballad. One reason for the decline of comic literary balladry in this century is the same as that for serious balladry of art, namely the disappearance of the folk and broadside ballads as widely familiar literary types. Then, too, most of the arts in the present age have tended toward the experimental to the partial neglect of the old forms. But the main reason is simply the dearth in our century of great British humorists.

Afterword

———•◦•———

THE purpose of this study has not been to make final pronouncements about the literary ballad but rather to chart a course through certain diverse and widely scattered materials, to assist the reader in making distinctions among poems superficially alike, and to provide a means of approach to a much-neglected genre.

A few concluding observations may now be made about the literary ballad as art. T. S. Eliot was right when he spoke of balladry as a form of verse, not necessarily of poetry, in which the clear presentation of the narrative was of first importance. The broadsides contain hardly any poetry at all. Thus our appreciation of an imitation broadside by Hardy or Auden depends more on our understanding of the poet's method than on the music or pictorial beauty of the poem. There is some poetry in the old folk ballads, but our primary response is to their romantic atmosphere and story. Part of the appeal of those literary ballads which are inspired by archaic folk models is embedded in our recollection of the older pieces and hence is partly outside the realm of poetry.

The literary ballad, then, is so closely bound to its tradition that it can never move far from it without becoming something else. This is in contrast to poems like "Tintern Abbey" or the "Ode to a Nightingale" or "Paradise Lost," which are unlimited in their possibilities of soaring imagination, originality, and beauty. The ballad is pretty largely earthbound even when it escapes into the supernatural; and it has to become more than a ballad, as "The Rime of the Ancient Mariner" does, before it can be classed among the greatest poems of English literature. Yet the perceptive audience for the greatest works of English poetry is far narrower than that for the vividly told stories in ballad form. And many of those who eventually learn to respond to the highest forms of poetic art are trained to this response through less ambitious poems like those we have been considering.

The literary ballad is perhaps unique among genres in being perfectly adaptable to all kinds of stories and situations, in standard English or in dialect, ancient or modern, light or serious. The genre has had special appeal for those poets who find significance in dramatic action, who are observers of events rather than probers of the mind, whose poetry tends to be direct and simple rather than subtle and complex. Thus it has appealed more to Scott than to Shelley, more to Housman than to Hopkins, more to Kipling than to Eliot. I could not deny that the literary balladists are more likely to be in the second than the first rank of poets. And if we must distinguish between poems we admire and those we love, the literary ballads would most frequently fall into the latter category. One can hardly compare a ballad with anything but another ballad. It is not usually philosophical or imagistic or cerebral; it is not concerned with the inner life of the artist or with subtlety of perception or observation. It is not often psychologically profound. We admit all these limitations and more. And yet when it is well done, the literary ballad deserves its permanent place in any collection of representative British poems. No finer means has ever been devised for the poetic presentation of short and dramatic narratives.

Appendix
Notes
Index

Appendix

A List of Literary Ballads

The following list of literary ballads is in no way definitive. Its purpose is simply to gather together and roughly classify several hundred titles as an indication of the scope and vitality of the genre. Few ballads earlier than 1750 are included, and most of those from the eighteenth century are to be found in Percy's *Reliques,* Lewis's *Tales of Wonder,* or Scott's *Minstrelsy.* In selecting the far larger number of nineteenth- and twentieth-century ballads, I have sought to include references to a) the best-known and most frequently anthologized pieces; b) ballads displaying variety in style and subject matter; and c) pieces of real poetic merit. While many minor authors are listed, I have frequently mentioned only one or two of their ballads. Numerous other minor balladists are omitted completely, especially if they made no real contribution to the genre. Better-known authors are more liberally treated; in general, I have attempted to list most of the ballads of the major figures. Many pieces have been omitted because they do not fit my definition of balladry, but the absence of any particular piece does not imply such a judgment upon it. What follows, in short, is a survey and not a census.

Since this study is not concerned with textual problems it has seemed unnecessary to give a source for each title. I have worked generally from an author's collected poems or from original editions. For some of the early minor poets, I have relied on the anthologists. The capital letter following each ballad title places it in one of the categories discussed in chapter 2.

TYPES OF LITERARY BALLADRY

A Ballads of the Supernatural
B Ballads of Tragedy
C Ballads of Love
D Ballads of Crime and Criminals
E Ballads of Scottish Border Life
F Ballads of War and Adventure
G Miscellaneous Ballads
H Humorous Ballads and Parodies

THE EIGHTEENTH CENTURY

Lady Anne Barnard (1750–1825)
　Auld Robin Gray (C).
Robert Burns (1759–96)
　The Battle of Sheriff-Muir (F); The Carle of Kellyburn Braes
　(H); John Barleycorn (H); Lady Mary Ann (C); The Lass
　that Made the Bed to Me (C); Last May a Braw Wooer (C);
　The Poor and Honest Sodger (C); A Waukrife Minnie (C);
　The Whistle (H).
Thomas Chatterton (1752–70)
　The Bristowe Tragedy (F).
William Cowper (1731–1800)
　The Diverting History of John Gilpin (H).
John Gay (1685–1732)
　Sweet William's Farewell to Black-Eyed Susan (C).
Richard Glover (1712–85)
　Admiral Hosier's Ghost (A).
Oliver Goldsmith (1728–74)
　Elegy on the Death of a Mad Dog (H); The Hermit, or Ed-
　win and Angelina (C).
Robert Lambe (1712–95)
　The Laidley Worm of Spindleston Heugh (A).
Hector MacNeill (1746–1818)
　Come Under My Plaidie (H); Donald and Flora (B); Mary

of Castlecary (C); My Boy Tammy (C); Oh, Tell Me How for to Woo (C).

David Mallet (1705?–65)
  Edwin and Emma (C); William and Margaret (A).

William Julius Mickle (1735–88)
  Hengist and May (B); The Sailor's Wife (C); The Sorceress (A).

Thomas Percy (1729–1811)
  The Child of Elle (C); The Friar of Orders Gray (C); The Hermit of Warkworth (C).

William Shenstone (1714–63)
  Jemmy Dawson (C).

Thomas Tickell (1686–1740)
  Lucy and Colin (C).

Lady Elizabeth Wardlaw (1677–1727)
  Hardyknute (F).

THE ROMANTIC PERIOD
(1798–1832)

Robert Allan (1774–1841)
  Lord Ronald Came to His Lady's Bower (B).

Joanna Baillie (1762–1851)
  The Elden Tree (B); The Ghost of Fadon (A); Lord John of the East (A); Malcolm's Heir (A); Sir Maurice (F).

William Blake (1757–1827)
  The Chimney Sweeper (in *Songs of Innocence*) (G); Fair Elenor (A); Gwin, King of Norway (A); A Poison Tree (G); William Bond (C).

George Gordon Byron (1788–1824)
  Alhama (F); The Black Friar (A); The Destruction of Sennacherib (F); The "Good Night" (G); Oscar of Alva (B).

Thomas Campbell (1777–1844)
  The Battle of the Baltic (F); Glenara (F); Lord Ullin's Daughter (C); The Wounded Hussar (C).

Samuel Taylor Coleridge (1772–1834)
  Ballad of the Dark Ladye (C); Love (C); The Rime of the Ancient Mariner (A); The Three Graves (A).

Allan Cunningham (1784-1842)
  The Bonnie Bairns (A); The Mermaid of Galloway (A).
Felicia Hemans (1793-1835)
  Casabianca (F); The Kaiser's Feast (G); The Landing of the Pilgrim Fathers (F).
James Hogg (The Ettrick Shepherd) (1770-1835)
  The Death of Douglas (E); Earl Walter (F); The Fray of Elibank (E); Gilmanscleuch (E); The Gude Greye Katt (H); Jock Johnstone the Tinkler (E); The Laird of Laristan, or The Three Champions of Liddesdale (E); The Liddel Bower (E); Lord Derwent (E); Lyttil Pynkie (A); The Mermaid (A); Mess John (A); The Pedlar (A); Sir David Graeme (B); The Witch of Fife (A).
Thomas Hood (1799-1845)
  The Dream of Eugene Aram (A); The Duel (H); Epping Hunt (H); Faithless Nelly Gray (H); Faithless Sally Brown (H); The Ghost (H); Jack Hall (H); John Day (H); John Jones (H); John Trot (H); The Last Man (D); Mary's Ghost (H); Pompey's Ghost (H); The Supper Superstition (H); Tim Turpin (H); A Waterloo Ballad (H).
Leigh Hunt (1784-1859)
  The Glove and the Lions (G).
John Keats (1795-1821)
  La Belle Dame Sans Merci (A).
Matthew Gregory Lewis (1775-1818)
  Alonzo the Brave and the Fair Imogine (A); The Bleeding Nun (A); Bothwell's Bonny Jane (A); The Cloud King (A); Courteous King Jamie (A); The Gay Gold Ring (A); Giles Jollup the Grave and Brown Sally Green (H); The Grim White Woman (A); Osric the Lion (A); The Sailor's Tale (H); Sir Guy the Seeker (A).
John Leyden, M.D. (1775-1811)
  The Cout of Keeldar (E); The Elfin King (A); The Lay of the Ettercap (H); Lord Soulis (E); The Mermaid (A).
William Maginn (1793-1842)
  The English Sailor and the King of Achen's Daughter (A); The Eve of St. Jerry (H); The Rime of the Auncient Waggonere (H).

John Marriott (1780–1825)
  Archie Armstrong's Aith (E).
Thomas Moore (1779–1852)
  By that Lake Whose Gloomy Shore (C); The High-Born Ladye (A); The Lake of the Dismal Swamp (A).
William Motherwell (1797–1835)
  Clerke Richard and Maid Margaret (C); The Ettin of Siller-wood (A); Elfinland Wud (A); The Fause Ladye (A); Halbert the Grim (A); Lord Archibald (A); The Master of Weemys (A); The Mermayden (A); Roland and Rosabelle (C); The Rose and the Fair Lilye (A); The Slayne Menstrel (E); True Love's Dirge (C).
Sir Walter Scott (1771–1832)
  Albert Graeme's Song (E); Alice Brand (A); Bonny Dundee (F); Cadyow Castle (E); The Castle of the Seven Shields (A); Christie's Will (E); Elspeth's Ballad (F); The Eve of St. John (A); The Fire King (A); Glenfinlas (A); Harold's Song (B); Jock of Haseldean (C); Kinmont Willie (?) (E); The Orphan Maid (G); Proud Maisie (A); Thomas the Rhymer III (A); Young Lochinvar (E).
Charles Kirkpatrick Sharpe (1781?–1851)
  The Murder of Caerlaveroc (B).
Percy Bysshe Shelley (1792–1822)
  The Fugitives (C); St. Edmond's Eve (A); Sister Rosa (A).
Robert Southey (1774–1843)
  The Battle of Blenheim (G); Bishop Bruno (A); Donica (A); God's Judgment on a Wicked Bishop (G); The Inchcape Rock (D); Jaspar (A); Lord William (A); Mary, the Maid of the Inn (B); The Old Woman of Berkeley (A); Queen Mary's Christening (G); Queen Orraca and the Five Martyrs of Morocco (A); Roprecht the Robber (D); Rudiger (A); The Surgeon's Warning (H); A True Ballad of St. Antidius, the Pope, and the Devil (A); The Well of St. Keyne (H).
William Robert Spencer (1769–1834)
  Beth Gêlert (G).
Robert Surtees (1779–1834)
  Barthram's Dirge (E); The Death of Featherstonehaugh (E); Lord Ewrie (E).

Henry Kirke White (1785–1806)
Gondoline (A).
Charles Wolfe (1791–1823)
The Burial of Sir John Moore (F).
William Wordsworth (1770–1850)
Alice Fell (G); Ellen Irwin (C); The Force of Prayer (B); George and Sarah Green (B); The Horn of Egremont Castle (F); The Last of the Flock (B); Lucy Gray (B); The Seven Sisters (B); We Are Seven (G).

THE VICTORIAN AGE
(1832–1890)

W. Harrison Ainsworth (1805–82)
The Barber of Ripon (H); Black Bess (D); The Custom of Dunmow (G); The Legend of the Lady of Rookwood (A); Old Grindrod's Ghost (H); The Old Oak Coffin (G).
William Allingham (1824–89)
The Faithless Knight (C); King Henry's Hunt (F); The Maids of Elfin-Mere (A); The Milkmaid (C); The Nobleman's Wedding (C); St. Margaret's Eve (A); The Witch-Bride (A).
Matthew Arnold (1822–88)
St. Brandan (A).
William Edmondstoune Aytoun (1813–65)
The Burial March of Dundee (F); The Execution of Montrose (F); The Heart of the Bruce (F); Little John and the Red Friar (H); The Massacre of the MacPherson (H); The Queen in France (H).
Richard Harris Barham (1788–1845)
The Babes in the Wood (H); A Lay of St. Nicholas (H); Misadventures at Margate (H); Nell Cook, a Legend of the Dark Entry (H).
John Stuart Blackie (1809–95)
The Emigrant Lassie (G); John Frazer (F); The Two Meek Margarets (F).
Stopford A. Brooke (1832–1916)
The King and the Huntsman (B).

Robert Browning (1812–89)
Hervé Riel (F); How They Brought the Good News from Ghent to Aix (F); Incident of the French Camp (F).

Robert W. Buchanan (1841–1901)
The Ballad of Judas Iscariot (A); The Ballad of Mary the Mother (A); The Battle of Drumliemoor (F); The Green Gnome (A); The Mermaid (H); Phil Blood's Leap (F).

Charles Stuart Calverley (1831–84)
First Love (H).

William Carleton (1794–1869)
Sir Turlough, or the Churchyard Bride (A).

Lewis Carroll (1832–98)
The Aged Aged Man (H); Father William (H); The Hunting of the Snark (H); Jabberwocky (H); The Lang Coortin' (H); The Two Brothers (H); The Walrus and the Carpenter (H); The Wandering Burgess (H).

Robert Chambers (1802–71)
Young Randal (H).

William Johnson Cory (1823–92)
A Ballad for a Boy (F).

Thomas Osborne Davis (1814–45)
Fontenoy (F); The Sack of Baltimore (F).

Aubrey DeVere (1814–1902)
A Ballad of Athlone (F); The Ballad of "Bonny Portmore" (F); A Ballad of Sarsfield (F); The Ballad of the Bier that Conquered (F).

Sydney Dobell (1824–74)
Daft Jean (B); Keith of Ravelston (A).

Austin Dobson (1840–1921)
The Ballad of "Beau Brocade" (D); The Mosque of the Caliph (G); My Landlady (B).

Sebastian Evans (1830–1909)
The Seven Fiddlers (A).

Richard Garnett (1835–1906)
The Highwayman's Ghost (D); The Mermaid of Padstow (A).

William Schwenck Gilbert (1836–1911)
Ellen McJones Aberdeen (H); Emily, John, James, and I

(H); Etiquette (H); General John (H); Gentle Alice Brown (H); Sir Guy the Crusader (H); The Story of Prince Agib (H); The Yarn of the "Nancy Bell" (H).

Alfred Perceval Graves (1846–1931)
Johnny Cox (F); The Sailor Girl (C); The Song of the Ghost (A).

Robert Stephen Hawker (1803–75)
Annot of Benallay (A); The Doom-Wall of St. Madron (A).

Mary Howitt (1799–1888)
The Boy of Heaven (A); The Fairies of the Caldon Low (A); An Old Man's Story (A); The Sin of Earl Walter (A); The Three Guests (A); The Voyage with the Nautilus (A).

Jean Ingelow (1820–97)
The High Tide on the Coast of Lincolnshire (B); Winstanley (G).

Charles Kingsley (1819–75)
Ballad of Earl Haldan's Daughter (C); Ballad: Lorraine, Lorraine, Lorree (B); The Knight's Leap (F); The Last Buccaneer (F); A New Forest Ballad (B); The Priest's Heart (A); The Sands o' Dee (B); Scotch Song (C); The Song of the Little Baltung (F); The Wierd Lady (B); The Young Knight (B).

Isa Craig Knox (1831–1903)
The Ballad of the Brides of Quair (C).

Frederick Locker-Lampson (1821–95)
Unfortunate Miss Bailey (H).

The Earl of Lytton ("Owen Meredith") (1831–91)
Aux Italiens (A).

George MacDonald (1824–1905)
Ballad of the Thulian Nurse (A); Janet (A); Legend of Corrievrechan (G); The Yerl o' Waterydeck (H).

Charles MacKay (1814–89)
The Kelpie of Corrievreckan (A); Tubal Cain (G).

Thomas B. Macaulay (1800–1859)
The Armada (F); The Battle of Naseby (F); Ivry: a Song of the Huguenots (F); The Last Buccaneer (A).

Gerald Massey (1828–1907)
Sir Richard Grenville's Last Fight (F).

George Meredith (1828–1909)

Archduchess Anne (C); Margaret's Bridal Eve (C); The Three Maidens (B); The Young Princess (B).

William Morris (1834–96)
Riding Together (F); The Sailing of the *Sword* (C); Shameful Death (F); Two Red Roses across the Moon (C); Welland River (C).

John Payne (1842–1916)
The Ballad of Isobel (A); May Margaret (A).

Thomas Love Peacock (1785–1866)
The Cauldron of Ceridwin (H); Llyn-Y-Dreiddiad-Vrawd; or, the Pool of the Diving Friar (H); The War-Song of Dinas Vawr (H).

Christina Georgina Rossetti (1830–94)
Love from the North (C); Maude Clare (C).

Dante Gabriel Rossetti (1828–82)
The Blessed Damozel (A); The King's Tragedy (B); My Sister's Sleep (B); Sister Helen (A); The Staff and Scrip (F); Stratton Water (C); Troy Town (G); The White Ship (B).

William Bell Scott (1811–90)
A Bridal Race (C); Glenkindie (G); A Lowland Witch Ballad (A); The Witch's Ballad (A); Woodstock Maze (B).

John Sterling (1806–44)
Alfred the Harper (F).

Robert Louis Stevenson (1850–94)
Heather Ale (G); Ticonderoga (A).

Algernon Charles Swinburne (1837–1909)
After Death (A); The Ballad of Dead Men's Bay (A); The Bloody Son (trans.) (B); The Bride's Tragedy (B); The Brothers (B); Burd Margaret (C); Duriesdyke (C); Earl Robert (B); The King's Daughter (B); Lord Scales (C); Lord Soulis (E); May Janet (C); The Sea Swallows (B); Westland Well (B); The Witch Mother (A); The Worm of Spindlestonheugh (A).

Alfred Tennyson (1809–92)
The Charge of the Light Brigade (F); Edward Gray (C); The Goose (H); King Charles's Vision (A); Lady Clare (C); The Lady of Shalott (B); The Lord of Burleigh (C); The Revenge (F); The Sisters (B).

William Makepeace Thackeray (1811–63)

The Ballad of Eliza Davis (H); Damages: Two Hundred Pounds (H); The Excellent New Ballad of Mr. Peel at Toledo (H); The Flying Duke (H); The King of Brentford's Testament (H); The Knight and the Lady (H); The Lamentable Ballad of the Foundling of Shoreditch (H); The Three Sailors (Little Billee) (H); The Willow Tree I (B); The Willow Tree II (H); A Woeful New Ballad of the Protestant Conspiracy to Take the Pope's Life (H); The Wofle New Ballad of Jane Roney and Mary Brown (H).

George Walter Thornbury (1828–76)
The Cavalier's Escape (F); Culloden (F); Old Sir Walter (F); The Three Troopers (F).

Henry Duff Traill (1810–89)
After Dilettante Concetti (H).

Oscar Wilde (1856–1900)
Ballade de Marguerite (B); The Ballad of Reading Gaol (D); The Dole of the King's Daughter (B).

THE MODERN PERIOD
(since 1890)

W. H. Auden (b. 1907)
As I Walked Out One Evening (C); Miss Gee (B); O the Valley in the Summer Where I and My John (C); The Quarry (G); Victor (B).

Alfred Austin (1835–1913)
At San Giovanni del Lago (G); Ave Maria (A); The Death of Huss (G); The Last Redoubt (F).

John Betjeman (b. 1906)
The Arrest of Oscar Wilde at the Cadogan Hotel (B); Death in Leamington (B); Exeter (H); A Subaltern's Love-song (C).

Robert Bridges (1844–1930)
Screaming Tarn (A).

John Davidson (1857–1909)
A Ballad of a Coward (F); A Ballad of a Nun (A); A Ballad of a Poet Born (G); A Ballad of a Workman (A); A Ballad of an Artist's Wife (A); A Ballad of Euthanasia (A); A Ballad of Heaven (A); A Ballad of Hell (A); The Last Ballad (C); A

New Ballad of Tannhauser (A).

Walter de la Mare (1873–1956)

The Ghost (A); The Silver Penny (B).

Padraic Gregory (b. 1886)

A Ballad of a Posthumous Child (B); The Ballad of Laird Gillie (A); The Ballad of Master Fox (B); The Ballad of the Ladye Lorraine (B); Fause Laird Forbes o' Tyne (E); The Ghost (A); The Lad the Fairies Stole (A); The Mad Son (B); The Water-Witch (A).

Thomas Hardy (1840–1928)

Ah, Are You Digging on My Grave? (A); At Shag's Heath (A); The Ballad of Love's Skeleton (C); The Brother (B); The Catching Ballet of the Wedding Clothes (C); The Dance at the Phoenix (G); The Dark-Eyed Gentleman (C); The Forbidden Banns (B); The Harvest Supper (A); Her Immortality (A); In the Days of Crinoline (C); Leipzig (F); The Lost Pyx (A); The Mock Wife (B); The Moth Signal (C); No Bell Ringing (A); The Pair He Saw Pass (A); The Peasant's Confession (F); A Practical Woman (G); The Rash Bride (B); The Ruined Maid (H); The Sacrilege (D); The Satin Shoes (B); The Second Night (A); The Slow Nature (B); A Sunday Morning Tragedy (B); The Supplanter (C); A Trampwoman's Tragedy (B); The Vampirine Fair (G); The Well-Beloved (A); The Widow Betrothed (C); The Workbox (B).

A. E. Housman (1859–1936)

Atys (B); Bredon Hill (B); The Carpenter's Son (B); The Culprit (D); The Deserter (F); Farewell to Barn and Stack and Tree (B); Grenadier (F); Is My Team Ploughing? (A); Lancer (F); The Merry Guide (A); New Year's Eve (G); Oh, Who Is That Young Sinner? (D); On Moonlit Heath (D); The True Lover (B); Oh See How Thick the Goldcup Flowers (C).

Rudyard Kipling (1865–1936)

The Ballad of Boh Da Thone (F); The Ballad of East and West (F); The Ballad of Fisher's Boarding House (F); The Ballad of Minepit Shaw (D); The Ballad of the "Bolivar" (F); The Ballad of the Cars (G); The Ballad of the "Clampherdown" (F); Cain and Abel (G); A Code of Morals (G); Danny Deever (F); Dinah in Heaven (A); Eddi's Service (A); The English Way (A); The Fall of Jock Gillespie (H); The Gift of the Sea (B); The Grave of the Hundred Head (F); Lament of the Border Cattle Thief (E); The Last of the Light Brigade (G); The Last Rhyme of True Thomas (A); The Last Suttee (G); Municipal (G); Our Lady of the Sackcloth (A); The Peace of Dives (G); Pink Dominoes (H); The Rhyme of the Three Captains (F); The Rhyme of the Three Sealers (F); Rimmon (G); The Sea Wife (A); Soldier, Solier (C); The Truce of the Bear (G).

Andrew Lang (1844–1912)

The Bridge of Death (B); The Fragment of the Fause Lover and the Dead Leman (A); The Milk-White Doe (A); Le Père Sévère (C); The Sudden Bridal (C); The Three Captains (G).

Louis MacNeice (1907–63)

The Streets of Laredo (G).

John Masefield (1878–1967)

Cap on Head (A); Cape Horn Gospel I (A); Cape Horn Gospel II (F); The Hounds of Hell (A); One of the Bo'sun's Yarns (F); The Yarn of the "Loch Achray" (B).

Edwin Muir (1887–1959)

Ballad of Everyman (A); Ballad of the Flood (A); Ballad of the Soul (A); The Enchanted Knight (A); The Voyage (A).

Alfred Noyes (1880–1958)

The Admiral's Ghost (A); Dick Turpin's Ride (D); The Highwayman (D); The Victory Ball (A); "Will Shakespeare's Out Like Robin Hood" (A).

William Plomer (b. 1903)

Anglo-Swiss: or, a Day Among the Alps (G); Atheling Grange: or, the Apotheosis of Lotte Nussbaum (A); The Dorking Thigh (G); French Lisette: a Ballad of Maida Vale (G); The Murder on the Downs (B); The Naiad of Ostend: or, a Fatal Passion (B); The Self-Made Blonde (B); A Shot in the Park (H); The Widow's Plot: or, She Got What Was Coming to Her (H).

Agnes Mary Frances Robinson (1857–1944)

Captain Gold and French Janet (C); The Mowers (C); Sir Eldric (A); The Tower of St. Maur (E).

William Soutar (1898–1943)
Ballad (B); The Tryst (C).

John M. Synge (1871–1909)
Danny (D); The 'Mergency Man (G); Patch-Shaneen (B).

Vernon Watkins (b. 1906)
Ballad of Crawley Woods (A); Ballad of Culver's Hole (D); Ballad of Hunt's Bay (A); Ballad of the Equinox (A); Ballad of the Rough Sea (A); Ballad of the Three Coins (A); Ballad of the Trial of Sodom (G); Ballad of the Two Tapsters (A).

William Butler Yeats (1865–1939)
The Ballad of Father Gilligan (A); The Ballad of Father O'Hart (G); The Ballad of the Foxhunter (B); The Ballad of Moll Magee (B); The Cap and Bells (A); Colonel Martin (G); The Host of the Air (G); Roger Casement (B).

Notes

———— ◦•◦ ————

I LITERARY BALLAD STYLES

1. The standard full-length analysis of British folk balladry is
Gordon Hall Gerould's *The Ballad of Tradition* (Oxford, 1932).
An excellent introductory study which emphasizes the folk bal-
lad but includes helpful discussions of the broadside ballad and
the literary ballad is Evelyn K. Wells's *The Ballad Tree* (New
York, 1950). The standard scholarly anthology of the older folk
balladry is that of Francis J. Child, *The English and Scottish
Popular Ballads,* 5 vols. (Boston and New York, 1882–98). The
Child collection is conveniently abridged in a one-volume edition,
English and Scottish Popular Ballads, ed. Helen Child Sargent
and George L. Kittredge (Boston, 1904). This contains excerpts
from Child's notes and repeats his numbering system, which is
widely used for ballad identification, e.g., "The Twa Sisters"
(Child no. 10).

The great editor of older broadside ballads was Hyder E.
Rollins of Harvard, whose edition of *The Pepys Ballads,* 8 vols.
(Cambridge, Mass., 1929–32), is an example of his meticulous
scholarship. His article "The Black-Letter Broadside Ballad,"
PMLA 34 (1919), 258–339, has not been superseded. A popu-
lar introduction which stresses the journalistic aspects of the
genre is Leslie Shepard's *The Broadside Ballad* (London, 1962).
This volume contains numerous photographic reproductions of
broadsides. Hundreds of ballads which originated as British
broadsides have found their way into tradition. Such pieces are
much more generally distributed and widely known than all
but a few of the Child ballads.

For references to ballads collected from tradition in Britain
and America, see for example Margaret Dean-Smith, *A Guide to
English Folk Song Collections* (Liverpool, 1954); Tristram P.
Coffin, *The British Traditional Ballad in North America,* rev. ed.

(Philadelphia, 1963); G. Malcolm Laws, Jr., *American Balladry from British Broadsides* (Philadelphia, 1957), and *Native American Balladry*, rev. ed. (Philadelphia, 1964). References to my numbering system appear occasionally in this study, e.g., "Captain Glen" (Laws no. K 22A).

Albert B. Friedman in *The Ballad Revival* (Chicago, 1961), has skillfully surveyed the multifarious involvements of literary men with balladry since the Elizabethan age. He refers to many literary ballads of the eighteenth, nineteenth, and twentieth centuries and discusses a number of them, but his broad plan of approach usually precludes detailed analysis. In this study I exclude ballad scholarship, collecting, and editing as topics of discussion unless they bear directly on the definition of analysis of the literary ballad as a distinct genre.

2. The best edition is *Reliques of Ancient English Poetry* by Thomas Percy, D.D., ed. Henry B. Wheatley, 3 vols. (London, 1886). This set is now available in a facsimile reprint, 3 vols. (New York, 1966). My references are to the Wheatley edition.

3. Aside from the *Reliques* and the *Minstrelsy*, the three anthologies which I have found most useful for their literary ballad texts are *The Pictorial Book of Old English Ballads*, ed. J. S. Moore (London, 1849); *Illustrated British Ballads*, ed. George Barnett Smith, 2 vols. (London, 1894); and *Popular British Ballads*, ed. R. Brimley Johnson, 4 vols. (London, 1894). All three are out of print, but a one-volume selection from Johnson's work is available in Everyman's Library (*A Book of British Ballads* [London, 1912]). This contains about fifty literary ballads as well as various folk and broadside pieces. *The Literary Ballad*, ed. Anne Henry Ehrenpreis, Arnold's English Texts (London, 1966), is a well-edited anthology of forty-one eighteenth- and nineteenth-century pieces.

4. *Minstrelsy, Ancient and Modern* (Glasgow, 1827), pp. 282–86; reprinted in Child, ed. Sargent and Kittredge, pp. 177–78.

5. *Poems and Translations, 1850–1870* (London, 1926), pp. 84–85.

6. "The Reiver's Wedding," *Complete Poetical Works* (Boston and New York, 1900), p. 30.

7. "Burd Margaret" in Algernon Charles Swinburne, *Ballads of the English Border*, ed. W. A. MacInnes (London, 1925), p. 120.

8. "The Water-Witch," *Collected Ballads of Padraic Gregory, 1912–1932* (London, 1935), pp. 39–40.

9. Text from Percy's *Reliques*, 3:172–76, with Percy's note: "Printed from two ancient copies, one of them in black letter in the Pepys Collection."

10. Addison wrote in part as follows:

> My Reader will think I am not serious, when I acquaint him that the piece I am going to speak of was the old Ballad of the *Two children in the Wood*, which is one of the darling Songs of the common people, and has been the delight of most *English-men* in some part of their age.
>
> This Song is a plain simple copy of nature, destitute of all the helps and ornaments of art. The tale of it is a pretty tragical story, and pleases for no other reason but because it is a copy of nature. There is even a despicable simplicity in the verse; and yet because the sentiments appear genuine and unaffected, they are able to move the mind of the most polite Reader with inward meltings of humanity and compassion.

The *Spectator*, no. 85, in *The Works of the Late Right Honorable Joseph Addison*, Esq., 4 vols. (Birmingham, 1761), 2:531.

11. *Reliques*, 3:241.
12. William Wordsworth and Samuel Taylor Coleridge, *Lyrical Ballads, 1798*, facsimile ed., ed. H. Littledale (Oxford, 1911), p. 137.
13. *The Collected Poems of A. E. Housman* (New York, 1940), p. 70.
14. Text from *Ballads and Tales*, vol. 20, Cornhill Edition of the *Works* (New York, 1923), 217.
15. From a broadside by J. Wrigley, Jr., Manchester; reprinted by Leslie Shepard, *The Broadside Ballad*, p. 159.
16. *Reliques*, 1:23.
17. Ibid., p. 40.
18. Text from *The Literary Ballad*, ed. Ehrenpreis, p. 37.
19. *Poetical Works*, 4th ed. (Boston, 1866), p. 104.
20. *Reliques*, 3:128–29.
21. *Poems* (London, 1907), pp. 228–29.
22. *Minstrelsy of the Scottish Border*, ed. T. F. Henderson, 4 vols. (Edinburgh, 1902), 4:290.
23. *Gertrude of Wyoming and Other Poems* (London, 1809), pp. 133–34; reprinted in Johnson, 4:146.
24. While the influence of the literary ballad on the folk and broadside ballad is outside the realm of this study, it has certainly been considerable. All ballads, of course, are "literary" in the sense that they are originally the work of individual authors composing within a tradition that has literary roots. The balladist of the streets has learned lessons from the balladry of the parlor and the music hall. And the humble folk composer who remains forever anonymous may differ more in opportunity than in talent from the mason (Allan Cunningham) or the shepherd (James Hogg) who becomes well known. Furthermore, a number of literary

ballads have worked their way into tradition by means of the broadside sheet and the songster. We can see in many broadside and folk ballads the expert use of well-established literary techniques.

2 LITERARY BALLAD SUBJECTS

1. "Modern Imitations of the Popular Ballad," *JEGP* 13 (1914), 88–98.
2. Francis J. Child, *The English and Scottish Popular Ballads*, 5 vols. (Boston, 1882–98), 2:200. Two stanzas of Mallet's ballad are given in chapter 3 and three more, along with parodies of them, in chapter 5.
3. See also Walter de la Mare, "The Ghost," *Collected Poems* (New York, 1941), pp. 93–94; Sydney Dobell, "Keith of Ravelston," reprinted in *Illustrated British Ballads*, 1:340–42; and Padraic Gregory, "The Ballad of Laird Gillie," *The Complete Collected Ballads of Padraic Gregory* (1912–32), (London, 1935), pp. 44–47.
4. *Collected Poems*, 4th ed. (London, 1930), p. 625.
5. "Her Immortality," *Collected Poems*, p. 49.
6. *Collected Poems*, p. 310.
7. *Rudyard Kipling's Verse: Definitive Edition* (New York, 1940), p. 96.
8. Allan Cunningham, ed., *The Songs of Scotland*, 4 vols. (London, 1825), 2:70–71. Reprinted in *Illustrated British Ballads*, ed. George B. Smith, 2 vols. (London, 1894), 1:85.
9. In a letter to T. Hall Caine quoted by Janet C. Troxell in *Rossetti's "Sister Helen"* (New Haven, 1939), p. 13.
10. *Rudyard Kipling's Verse*, p. 380. Reprinted by Evelyn K. Wells in *The Ballad Tree* (New York, 1950), pp. 342–46. Miss Wells discusses the poem on p. 322.
11. See Sir Walter Scott, *Minstrelsy of the Scottish Border*, ed. T. F. Henderson, 4 vols. (Edinburgh, 1902, 4:277 ff.
12. R. H. Cromek, *Remains of Nithsdale and Galloway Song* (London, 1810).
13. Ibid., p. 246.
14. The relationships between German and English literary balladry in the late eighteenth and early nineteenth centuries are complex and unclear, but it seems generally agreed that the German ballad movement was first inspired by Percy's *Reliques*. We also have Walter Scott's testimony that the German literary ballad was the first source of poetic inspiration for him. The literary ballads of Scott and M. G. Lewis were in their turn influential in Germany, and both old and new works of the German balladists continued to be popular in nineteenth-century England.

15. Bürger's ballad is related in motif to "The Suffolk Miracle" (Child no. 272), in which the dead lover's ghost takes the girl on a midnight horseback ride. Taylor's text is reprinted in Lewis's *Tales of Wonder* (1801). The translators generally altered Burger's strange and headlong meter, which goes like this:

> Schön Liebchen schürzte, sprang und schwang
> Sich auf das Ross behende;
> Wohl um den trauten Reiter schlang
> Sie ihre Lilienhände;
> Und hurre, hurre, hopp, hopp, hopp!
> Gings fort in sausendem Galopp,
> Dass Ross und Reiter schnoben
> Und Kies und Funken stoben.

From *Deutsche Balladen*, ed. Hans Fromm (Krefeld, 1953), p. 50.

16. From *Tales of Wonder*, ed. M. G. Lewis, 2 vols. (Dublin, 1801), 1:210. Browning may have had this or a similar passage in the back of his mind when he wrote stanza 21 of "Childe Roland to the Dark Tower Came":

> Which, while I forded,—good saints, how I feared
>   To set my foot upon a dead man's cheek,
>   Each step, or feel the spear I thrust to seek
> For hollows, tangled in his hair or beard!
> —It may have been a water-rat I speared,
>   But, ugh! it sounded like a baby's shriek.

(*The Works of Robert Browning*, Centenary Edition, 10 vols. [London, 1912], 3:410).

17. Parodies of horror balladry are briefly discussed in chapter 5.

18. "The Forsaken Merman" has been included among the literary ballads by some anthologists, but it seems to me too remote from ballad form and style.

19. *The Complete Poetical Works of Robert Buchanan*, 2 vols. (London, 1901), 2:494–96. Reprinted in *Popular British Ballads*, ed. R. Brimley Johnson, 4 vols. (London, 1894), 4:79.

20. *Rudyard Kipling's Verse*, p. 516.

21. *Collected Poems*, p. 158. In a note Hardy explains that the place referred to is "Cross-in-Hand," which he connects with another local legend in *Tess of the d'Urbervilles*.

22. *Collected Poems* (London, 1960), p. 32.

23. *Rudyard Kipling's Verse*, p. 373.

24. See group "M" in my *American Balladry from British Broadsides* (Philadelphia, 1957).

25. "Swinburne and the Popular Ballad," *PMLA* 49 (1934), 295–309.

26. Algernon Charles Swinburne, *Ballads of the English Border*, ed. W. A. MacInnes (London, 1925), pp. 143–44.
27. For various ballads of this kind in tradition see *American Balladry from British Broadsides*, nos. N 28–N 43.
28. See "My Bonny Black Bess II," *American Balladry from British Broadsides*, p. 170.
29. See "My Bonny Black Bess I," *American Balladry from British Broadsides*, p. 169.
30. For an account of the early nineteenth-century ballad trade, see Charles Hindley, *The Life and Times of James Catnach (Late of Seven Dials), Ballad Monger* (London, 1878).
31. See chapter 1.
32. The term "border ballad" is loosely used by poets and anthologists to mean, for example, a) ballads dealing specifically with border raids, b) folk ballads in the Scottish dialect, or c) ballads originating on either side of the border. William Beattie's *Border Ballads* (Hammondsworth, Middlesex, 1952), uses the term as Scott did to mean traditional Scottish texts of varied subject matter from border country.
33. Child, 3:477.
34. In my opinion, the following facts, when taken together, establish Scott as the author: (1) No collected text of "Kinmont Willie" has been reported from among Scott's carefully preserved materials for the *Border Minstrelsy* or from any other source; (2) the hero of the ballad is Sir Walter Scott of Branxholm, an ancestor of the famous writer; (3) every important detail of the story can be found either in the two related ballads or in a prose account of the event by a contemporary writer; (4) where the language departs from that of the other ballads, it is patently literary; and (5) Scott himself admitted having emended the text before publishing it in the *Minstrelsy*. Various writers have hesitated to accuse Scott of outright duplicity in this matter. Perhaps it would be better to regard it as a form of practical joke. For other conclusions and references, see S. B. Hustvedt, *Ballad Books and Ballad Men* (Cambridge, Mass., 1930), chapter 2; and T. F. Henderson's edition of the *Minstrelsy*, 2:57.
35. *Minstrelsy*, 4:72.
36. Ibid., p. 190.
37. "The Death of Douglas," *The Works of the Ettrick Shepherd*, 2 vols. (London, 1869), 2:79.
38. Ibid., p. 342.
39. William C. DeVane reports that Browning received one hundred guineas for this poem from *Cornhill Magazine* in 1871 and donated his receipts for the relief of the Parisians, whose city had fallen to the Prussians. (*A Browning Handbook*, 2nd, ed.

[New York, 1955], p. 407.) This is probably the record price for a literary ballad.

40. Dean DeVane, who notes this similarity, says that the fame of the two poems is comparable.

41. *Poems by Gerald Massey*, 6th ed. (Boston, 1866), pp. 419–23.

42. *Gertrude of Wyoming and Other Poems* (London, 1809), pp. 108–13. Reprinted in Johnson, 3:146–49.

43. *Rudyard Kipling's Verse*, p. 135.

44. For examples of such pieces, see William M. Doerflinger, *Shantymen and Shantyboys: Songs of the Sailor and Lumberman* (New York, 1951).

45. The largest class of battle ballads lies outside the scope of this volume. These are found among the songs and ballads written by Irish poets of the mid-nineteenth century and later, who tried to inspire their countrymen with the glories of Ireland's past. Their avowed motives were propagandistic, and their ballads, some of which were first published in the periodical *The Nation*, were ultimately designed to assist in establishing Irish independence. One of the great anthologies of such pieces is Charles Gavan Duffy's *The Ballad Poetry of Ireland*, which was first published in Dublin in 1845 and had reached its thirty-ninth edition by 1866. Duffy was founder and coeditor with Thomas O. Davis of *The Nation*, and Davis was one of its leading ballad writers. The history of Anglo-Irish literary balladry has yet to be written.

46. *The Oxford Book of English Verse*, new ed. (Oxford, 1939), p. 175.

47. *Songs of the Cavaliers and Roundheads* (London, 1857), p. 132.

48. *Poems of W. E. Aytoun* (Oxford, 1921), pp. 34–35.

3 THE ARCHAIC LITERARY BALLAD

1. *English and Scottish Ballads* (London, 1957), pp. xxiv–xxv.

2. London, 1791.

3. *Reliques*, ed. Henry B. Wheatley, 3 vols. (London, 1876–77), 1:xxxii.

4. Text from *Reliques*, 3:310.

5. Reprinted as "Lord George and Lady Dorothy" in Thomas Evans's *Old Ballads*, 4 vols. (London, 1810), 3:354.

6. Reprinted in *Popular British Ballads*, ed. R. Brimley Johnson, 4 vols. (London, 1894), 3:1–8.

7. Text from *Reliques*, 1:243–44.

8. "Essay on Imitations of the Ancient Ballad," *Minstrelsy of the Scottish Border*, ed. T. F. Henderson, 4 vols. (Edinburgh, 1902), 4:48.

9. *Poetical Works* (New York, 1839), pp. 473–75.
10. Ibid., p. 435.
11. For an enlightening analysis see Tristram P. Coffin, "Coleridge's Use of the Ballad Stanza in *The Rime of the Ancient Mariner*," *MLQ*, 12 (1951), 437–45. The ballad qualities of the poem are also discussed by Albert Friedman in *The Ballad Revival* (Chicago, 1961), pp. 277–82.
12. Text from *The Poems*, ed. E. H. Coleridge (London, 1935), pp. 186–209, with the exception of the stanza cited in note 13.
13. *Lyrical Ballads, 1798,* facsimile ed., ed. H. Littledale (Oxford, 1911), p. 18.
14. Text from the *Minstrelsy*, 4:161–72.
15. *The Works of the Ettrick Shepherd*, 2 vols. (London, 1869), 2: 84–86.
16. *Poetical Works*, 4th ed. (Boston, 1866), pp. 258–59.
17. Edward, Lord Lytton, trans., *Schiller's Poems and Ballads* (London, 1887), pp. 20–21.
18. *The Collected Poems, Lyrical and Narrative, of A. Mary F. Robinson (Madame Duclaux)* (London, 1902), pp. 265–71. Reprinted in Johnson, 4:118–26.
19. Swinburne's "Itylus" is based on the legend of Procne, her husband Tereus, and her sister Philomela. When Procne learns that Tereus has violated Philomela, she gets revenge by killing her son Itylus and feeding his body to his father.
20. Algernon Charles Swinburne, *Ballads of the English Border*, ed. W. A. MacInnes (London, 1925), pp. 167–69. Reprinted in Johnson, 4:43–45.
21. Clyde K. Hyder, "Swinburne and the Popular Ballad," *PMLA* 49 (1934), 295–309.
22. *English and Scottish Popular Ballads*, ed. Sargent and Kittredge (Boston, 1904), p. 173.
23. *Ballads of the English Border*, pp. 131–32, 134.
24. Ibid., pp. 197–98.
25. From "Address on the Collection of Paintings of the English Pre-Raphaelite School . . . 1891," reprinted in *William Morris: Artist, Writer, Socialist*, ed. May Morris, 2 vols. (Oxford, 1936), 1:298–303.
26. *The Collected Works of William Morris*, 24 vols. (London and New York, 1910–15), 1:103.
27. *Dante Gabriel Rossetti*, Writers and Their Work, no. 85 (London, 1957), p. 15.
28. Text from *Poems and Translations, 1850–1870* (London, 1926), pp. 76–83.
29. *Rossetti's "Sister Helen"* (New Haven, 1939).

4 THE CONTEMPORARY LITERARY BALLAD

1. Text from Percy's *Reliques,* ed. Henry B. Wheatley, 3 vols. (London, 1876–77), 1:328–31.
2. Selected and arranged by D. B. Wyndham Lewis and Charles Lee (New York, 1930).
3. "Hart-Leap Well," *The Poetical Works of Wordsworth,* ed. Thomas Hutchinson, Oxford Standard Edition (New York, n.d.), p. 202.
4. Ibid., pp. 82–83.
5. See Wordsworth's Preface of 1800, *Lyrical Ballads, 1798,* facsimile ed., ed. H. Littledale (Oxford, 1911), p. 249.
6. *The Ballad Revival* (Chicago, 1961) p. 272.
7. That the poems which appeared in the *Lyrical Ballads* of 1798 were actually quite conventional in subject matter and treatment, though above average in quality, is shown by Robert Mayo in "The Contemporaneity of the *Lyrical Ballads,*" *PMLA* 69 (1954), 486–552. Professor Mayo impressively demonstrates Wordsworth's debt to the contemporary poetry of the magazines and miscellanies, which was itself partly of broadside descent. It may also be observed that very few of Wordsworth's early attempts to write in the simple manner of everyday speech are now regarded as worth anthologizing. The first edition of *Lyrical Ballads* consists largely of unfamiliar titles.
8. Text from *Reliques,* 2:371–74.
9. *The Poems of Robert Burns* (Oxford, 1903), p. 495.
10. *Collected Poems,* 4th edition (London, 1930), p. 227.
11. *Poems,* p. 513.
12. From "Rudyard Kipling," *On Poetry and Poets* (New York, 1957), pp. 268–69. Originally published in *A Choice of Kipling's Verse* (London, 1941).
13. *Rudyard Kipling's Verse: Definitive Edition* (New York, 1940), p. 57.
14. Ibid., p. 234.
15. *John Betjeman's Collected Poems* (London, 1958), pp. 98–99.
16. *The Collected Poems of A. E. Housman* (New York, 1940), p. 20.
17. See C. R. Baskervill, "English Songs on the Night Visit," *PMLA* 36 (1921), 565–614.
18. *Collected Poems,* pp. 78–79.
19. *Collected Poems,* p. 36.
20. *Selected Poems of Thomas Hardy* (New York, 1961), p. xxix.
21. *Collected Poems,* p. 724.
22. Ibid., p. 840.

23. Ibid., pp. 773–74.
24. Ibid., p. 882.
25. *Collected Shorter Poems, 1927–1957* (New York, 1966), pp. 109–12.
26. Ibid., pp. 112–17. The first two stanzas of "Victor" are reminiscent in style and substance of the Negro ballad "John Henry." Thus Auden's unheroic Victor invites ironic comparison with the heroic and self-sufficient steel driver. Both "Victor" and "Miss Gee" are arranged under the general heading "Songs and other musical pieces," another reminder of the relationship between literary balladry and folksong.
27. *The Collected Poems of Louis MacNeice*, ed. E. R. Dodds (New York, 1967), pp. 217–18.

5 HUMOROUS LITERARY BALLADS AND PARODIES

1. *The Humorous Verse of Lewis Carroll* (New York, 1960), pp. 214, 221.
2. Ibid., pp. 258–59. The ballad can be understood with the aid of a note provided on p. 254.
3. *The Book of Ballads, Edited by Bon Gaultier*, new ed. (Edinburgh, 1904), pp. 135–38. This edition contains a delightful preface written by Sir Theodore Martin at the age of eighty-seven, which provides much helpful information about the origin and authorship of the poems which he and Aytoun wrote.
4. Ibid., p. 200.
5. Ibid.
6. *The Humorous Verse of Lewis Carroll*, p. 32.
7. *Rudyard Kipling's Verse: Definitive Edition* (New York, 1940), pp. 64–65.
8. *Tales of Terror and Wonder*, ed. Henry Morley (London, 1887), pp. 81–83.
9. M. G. Lewis, ed. *Tales of Wonder*, 2 vols. (Dublin, 1801), 1:70–75.
10. *Tales of Terror and Wonder*, pp. 56–59.
11. *The Odoherty Papers of the Late William Maginn*, ed. Shelton Mackenzie, 2 vols. (New York, 1855), 1:101–5.
12. *A Century of Parody and Imitation*, ed. Walter Jerrold and R. M. Leonard (Oxford, 1913), p. 350.
13. *The Ingoldsby Legends* (London, 1906), p. 422.
14. *Modern Street Ballads*, ed. John Ashton (London, 1888), p. 126.
15. From a review of Southey's *Thalaba, the Destroyer*, *The Edinburgh Review* (October 1802). Reprinted in *Early Reviews of Great Writers* (1786–1832), ed. E. Stevenson (London, n.d.), p. 31.

16. *The Complete Poetical Works*, ed. H. S. Milford (London, 1907), pp. 346–47. Reprinted in *Popular British Ballads*, ed. R. Brimley Johnson, 4 vols. (London, 1894), 3.
17. *The Complete Poetical Works* (New York, 1866), pp. 323–25. Reprinted in Johnson, 3.
18. Reprinted in *The Humorous Poetry of the English Language*, ed. James Parton (Boston, 1884), p. 475.
19. *Ballads and Tales*, vol. 20 of the Cornhill Edition of the *Works* (New York, 1923), 229.
20. *The Bab Ballads*, 4th ed. (London, 1899), pp. 101, 105.
21. *Ballads and Tales*, p. 187.

Index

The numbers in parentheses following a ballad title are those used in Francis J. Child's *The English and Scottish Popular Ballads* (Boston, 1882–98) and in my *American Balladry from British Broadsides* (Phila., 1957). The titles of many literary ballads not listed in this Index will be found under their authors' names in the Appendix, pp. 149–61.